Key Concepts in the Practice of

SUFISM

Emerald Hills of the Heart

4

Key Concepts in the Practice of

SUFISM

Emerald Hills of the Heart

4

M. Fethullah Gülen

Translated by Ali Ünal

TUGHRA
BOOKS

New Jersey

Published by Tughra Books

345 Clifton Ave., Clifton,

NJ, 07011, USA

www.tughrabooks.com

Library of Congress Cataloging-in-Publication Data Available

ISBN (paperback): 978-1-59784-228-0
ISBN (hardcover): 978-1-59784-213-6

Printed by
Çağlayan A.Ş., İzmir - Turkey

TABLE OF CONTENTS

Preface: M. Fethullah Gülen & *Emerald Hills Of The Heart* vii

Talib, Murid, Salik, Wasil (The Seeker, The One Who Wills,
    The Initiate, The One Who Has Attained or Reached)........................... 1

The Initiate from a Different Perspective.................................... 14

Wasil (One Who Has Attained or Reached)................................... 24

Khushu and *Hurma* (Reverent Awe and Respect)........................ 38

The Horizon of "the Secret" and What Lies Beyond................. 47

Haqq (The Truth), *Haqiqa* (The Genuine) and What Lies Beyond 56

God and the Truth of Divinity 62

Metaphysical Realms 75

    The *'Arsh* (The Supreme Throne of God)................................. 75

    The *Kursiyy* (The Supreme Seat of God)................................. 83

    Sidratu'l-Muntaha (The Lote-Tree of the Furthest Limit)............... 88

    Al-Baytu'l-Ma'mur (The Prosperous House) 90

Lawhun Mahfuz (The Supreme Preserved Tablet) and What Lies Before..........93

(*Ta'ayyunat*) Identifications and What Lies Before.................... 103

God's Attributes of Glory 115

    The Divine Attributes from the Perspective of the Essentials
    or Basic Foundations of the Religion............................. 124

The Attributes in the Negative or the Attributes of
    Exemption or Freedom.. 124

The Essential Attributes.. 126

    Wujud ([The All-Holy, Self-]Existence)......................... 126

    Wahdaniyya (Oneness).. 127

    Qidam (Having No Beginning) 129

    Baqa (Eternal Permanence).. 129

    Muhalafatun lil-Hawadith (Being Unlike the Created)............. 131

    Qiyam bi-Nafsihi (Self-Subsistence) 132

The Positive or Affirmative Attributes 132

   Hayah (Life) 133

   'Ilm (Knowledge)... 134

   Sam'a (Hearing) 136

   Basar (Sight).. 137

   Irada (Will)... 138

   Qudra (Power) 140

   Kalam (Speech)... 141

   Takwin (Making Exist) 143

The Attributes of Action... 144

   Khalq (Creation) 144

   Ibda' (Originating Uniquely) 146

   Insha' (Producing) 146

   Ihya' and Imata (Giving Life and Reviving, and Causing to Die).. 147

   Tarziq (Providing)... 148

God's Figurative Attributes.. 149

The All-Beautiful Names of God 154

The Names Indicating the Divine Essence 168

The Names Originating in Divine Attributes of Glory..................... 170

The Names Indicating Divine Acts 171

The Foundational Names 173

The Names of Majesty.. 174

The Names of Grace... 174

Putting an End to a Long Journey 175

Bibliography... 191

Index.. 195

PREFACE

M. FETHULLAH GÜLEN &
EMERALD HILLS OF THE HEART

T his book is the 4th or last of the series of *Emerald Hills of the Heart: Key Concepts in the Practice of Sufism* by M. Fethullah Gülen.

Fethullah Gülen, reverently called Hojaefendi and known for his simple and austere lifestyle, profound learning, and education and interfaith dialogue activities, is a scholar of remarkable proportions. He was born in Erzurum, eastern Turkey, in 1941. Upon graduation from divinity school, he obtained his license to preach and teach. His social reform efforts, begun during the 1960s, have made him one of Turkey's most well-known and respected public figures and gained him a universal reputation as a peace, education and dialogue activist.

Though simple in outward appearance, he is original in thought and action. He embraces all humanity, and is deeply averse to unbelief, injustice, and deviation. His belief and feelings are profound, and his ideas and approach to problems are both wise and rational. A living model of love, ardor, and feeling, he is balanced in his thoughts, acts, and treatment of matters.

He is acknowledged, either tacitly or explicitly, by Turkish intellectuals and scholars as one of the most serious and important thinkers and writers, and among the wisest activists of twentieth-century Turkey or even of the entire world. But such accolades do not deter him from striving to be no more than a humble servant of God and a friend to all. Desire for fame is the same as show and ostentation, a "poisonous honey" that extinguishes the heart's spiritual liveliness: is one of the golden rules he follows.

After completing his education, Fethullah Gülen first taught in Edirne, a province in the west border of Turkey with Europe, and was active in religious and social services. After doing his military service and teaching for some time in Edirne, he was transferred to İzmir, which proved to be a turning-point in his life. It was during this time that his total dedication to religious life and his interest in the general human condition became apparent. While in İzmir, he began to travel from city to city to speak on various religious and social subjects, and to visit places where people gathered to convey his message.

Gülen dreamed of a generation that would combine intellectual "enlightenment" with pure spirituality, wisdom, and continuous activism. Being notably knowledgeable in religious and social sciences and familiar with the principles of "material" sciences, he instructed his students in most of these areas. The first students who attended his courses in İzmir became the vanguard of a revived generation willing to serve his ideals.

Fethullah Gülen unequivocally believes and asserts that if you wish to serve people in the best way possible, simply make them thirst knowledge and equip them with love and self-sacrifice or altruism. "One who wants to live should first try to make others live," is one of the primary principles he follows. Dedicated to solving society's problems, he maintains that the road to justice for all is paved with adequate universal education which aims at both intellectual and spiritual enlightenment, for only this will engender a sufficient level of understanding and dialogue in the society for the rights of others. To this end, he has encouraged society's elite and community leaders, industrialists, and business leaders in his community to support quality education for the needy.

Gülen is well-known for his ardent endeavor to strengthen bonds among people. He maintains that there are more bonds bringing people together than those separating them. Based on this belief, he works without rest for a sincere, sound dialogue and mutual understanding. He was one of the founders of the Foundation of Journalists and Writers, a group that promotes dialogue and understanding both in Turkey and abroad. Gülen envisions a twenty-first century in which we will see the sprouting of a spiritual dynamic that will revive the now-dormant moral values. He envisions an age of dialogue and understanding that will lead to the cooperation of civilizations and their ultimate fusion into one body. The human spirit shall triumph in the form of intercivilizational dialogue and the sharing of values.

"As for getting others to accept your ways," Fethullah Gülen tells us, "the days of getting things done by brute force are over. In today's world, the only way to get others to accept your ideas is by persuasion and convincing arguments. Those who resort to brute force to reach their goal are intellectually bankrupt souls." In their daily lives, people must maintain the delicate balance between material and spiritual values if they are to enjoy serenity and true happiness. Unbridled greed must be guarded against. He continues to feel, deeply and inwardly, the suffering of both humanity's intellectual and spiritual bankruptcy and of those who are oppressed by the prevailing materialistic worldview. A true guide who leads by example, he lives as he preaches and presents an ideal living model to emulate. A student of *hadith, tafsir, fiqh,* Sufism, and philosophy, he occupies his rightful place among his contemporaries in Islamic sciences.

He has taught many scholarly people, and continues to teach in private. His sermons and discourses have been recorded on thousands of tapes and video cassettes, and many books have been compiled from his articles, sermons, and the answers he has given to different questions over the years. Some of his books are as follows:

- *Asrın Getirdiği Tereddütler* (4 volumes; vols. I and II have appeared as *Questions and Answers about Islam*)
- *Kalbin Zümrüt Tepeleri* (4 volumes; translated as *Emerald Hills of the Heart: Key Concepts in the Practice of Sufism*)
- *Çağ ve Nesil* ("This Era and the Young Generation")

- *Ölçü veya Yoldaki Işıklar*, (4 volumes; vol. 1 has appeared as *Pearls of Wisdom*)
- *Zamanın Altın Dilimi* ("The Golden Part of Time")
- *Renkler Kuşağında Hakikat Tomurcukları* (2 volumes; vol. 1 has appeared as *Truth through Colors*)
- *Kırık Mızrap* ("Broken Plectrum"), a collection of verse
- *Fatiha Üzerine Mülahazalar* ("The Interpretation of Sura-tu'l-Fatiha")
- *Sonsuz Nur* (2 volumes, translated as *Muhammad: The Messenger of God*)
- *Yitirilmiş Cennet'e Doğru* (translated as *Towards the Lost Paradise*)
- *İnancın Gölgesinde* (translated as *The Essentials of Islamic Faith*)
- Some of Hodjaefendi's books, such as *Kırık Mızrap*, *İnancın Gölgesinde*, *Sonsuz Nur,* and *Asrın Getirdiği Tereddütler* have also been translated into many other languages such as German, Russian, Albanian, and Bulgarian.

EMERALD HILLS OF THE HEART – KEY CONCEPTS IN THE PRACTICE OF SUFISM

The aspect of Fethullah Gülen's "mission" or personality as a trainer of the human soul may be seen most profoundly and comprehensively in *Emerald Hills of the Heart*, a four-volume compilation of his writings that were published over the years in the monthly periodical, *Sızıntı*. In this series, Gülen introduces and describes the various stages of the Sufi path or elucidates the principles of Sufism; to be more exact, he portrays the spiritual and moral facets of Islam. This is done via a conceptual framework. Those who follow the articles can immediately see that this enunciation or style of analysis of the subject is different from the methods followed by others who have laid emphasis on Sufi concepts.

Those readers who are not familiar with Islam or Sufism should notice the following points.

First, men and women begin to follow the Sufi path when they sense there is something more to Islam than what appears on the surface or that they should get nearer to God. They act on this desire by following a stricter way of self-purification in order to penetrate the "inner" dimension and meaning of Islamic rituals, to reach a deeper understanding of the meaning and purposes of the Divine Acts, and to acquire thereby knowledge and love of Him. When this point has been reached, God begins to draw them to Himself at a pace appropriate for that particular individual. With the help of a spiritual guide, who does not force but rather only suggests and clarifies matters for the aspirant, the novice Sufi begins the journey back to God by means of the instructions and techniques required for progressing on the path. As the aspirant's will becomes ever-closer aligned with God's Will, it is the individual Sufi who freely chooses to progress further. There is no external force or pressure.

Sufism does not consist of only obeying orders, submitting to a spiritual leader, engaging in constant self-criticism sessions, and employing various methods to "reform" or "cleanse" one's character or mind. It is not a "cult," in the current pejorative sense that this term has acquired in the West. Although these elements are present in Sufism, no one is predestined or commanded to engage in them. One cannot be coerced into following the Sufi path by threats or promises, whether made by God or another Sufi. God is not a "master" who demands that His "slaves" follow this path – or else. He does not order individuals to do what is impossible for them and then punish them when they cannot comply with His "demand."

But, most important of all, Sufism is a life-long process of spiritual development. The reader will notice throughout this series that each stage or station is a gift of God. This does not mean, however, that the aspirant can sit back and wait for it to be bestowed. Quite the contrary: An individual must actively prepare himself or herself to receive the gift through the method given by his or her spiritual guide. When the individual has accomplished this, the gift will be bestowed.

Second, the author emphasizes such concepts as human innate poverty and powerlessness. These concepts have specific meanings in Sufism, all of which stem from the belief that God is the source of everything. For example, one cannot have true power because all power belongs to God. Therefore, in reality he or she is powerless. One is helpless, because there is no one who can provide assistance other than God. One's perception and admittance of helplessness and destitution before God, the source of everything, is the real source of his or her power and wealth. An individual is powerful by the Power of God, and wealthy by the Richness of God.

Understood in this context, one sees immediately that Sufism is a path demanding the individual's active participation in his or her spiritual growth and development. One is not allowed to be passive, hoping that God will bestow this or that blessing or station. Rather, one does what is necessary to grow spiritually, and God bestows the blessings and stations when the individual is ready to receive them.

Emerald Hills of the Heart, from one vantage point, erects a framework, while from another vantage point it abolishes all limits and frames. As the spiritual life has more of an "esoteric" nature and as proceeding on the "esoteric" track is both difficult and extremely strenuous, such a journey must be undertaken within a specific framework. Bediüzzaman Said Nursi, a twentieth- century Turkish scholar and reviver, warns that all the factions that have digressed (on the Sufi path) have been led astray by leaders who have set out into the inner dimension of existence, who for a moment made progress, but because they did not comply with the Sunna, presumed that what they had received meant that they had reached the apex, and thus regressed, misleading both themselves and others. Since journeying on the spiritual path is risky and this path contains many special characteristics, those who enter it must observe the principles of Islamic jurisprudence strictly and try to advance in the lights it provides in order to be able to avoid possible deviances. Throughout history, stemming from partial ignorance or neglect of these principles, or simply from dissociation with them due to some theoretical considerations, many Sufi sects, deceptive in their esoteric inclinations, have emerged, while many other deviant sects or factions have sought a safe haven under the protection of Sufism. Hence, for spiritual or Sufi life to advance on the basis of Islamic principles or along the guidelines of Islamic jurisprudence without causing or suffering any digressions, *Emerald Hills of the Heart* delineates the limits of the spiritual path, illuminating it at the same time with floodlit projectors that it has placed at every stage and station.

While sketching such limits, *Emerald Hills of the Heart*, as we have indicated, destroys all limits and borders imposed before the spiritual journeying. Such a spiritual progression is virtually infinite, and is comprised of as many stages and ranks as there are believers, from the most honorable of all creation, the Prophet Muhammad, upon him be peace and blessings, to the most ordinary Muslim. Furthermore, although on the one hand this path is accessible to all, from another perspective it has particular lanes, along which only very few humans are able to walk. The school of Muhyi'd-Din ibnu'l-'Arabi, or the doctrine of *Wahdatu'l-Wujud*, which literally means "the Transcendental Unity of Being," for instance, may be considered to be among the most particular of these lanes. The spiritual path also contains various distinguishing subtle characteristics or particularities that can only be comprehended by those with the ability to brave these rough terrains. *Emerald Hills of the Heart,* however, is able to evaluate these characteristics within both the boundaries and limits of the Islamic measures and the enormous profundity and infinity of spiritual life.

Emerald Hills of the Heart also presents God through all His Attributes and Names, thus profusely illuminating the way. This feature allows for the sciences of theology, Sufism and wisdom, or *Hikmah*, as it is termed in Islam, which is different from philosophy, to emerge from within *Emerald Hills of the Heart* as a science of *Ma'rifah*, or knowledge of God. These sciences in unison expound a detailed synoptic map of the Divine manifestation and the relationship between the Creator and the created, which are often alluded to in Islamic Sufism in the shade of certain mysterious symbols and expressions that are difficult to comprehend. In addition, both through the concepts and subjects mentioned and certain other concepts and subjects it discusses such as "Heavenly Realms," "Metaphysical Realms," "Archetypes and the World of Representations or Ideal Forms," *Emerald Hills of the Heart* presents ontology and draws a metaphysical roadmap that can shed a light on physics and astrophysics. In addition to these, by way of utilizing such spiritual ranks as *Talib* (the Seeker), *Murid* (the One Who Wills), *Salik* (the Initiate), and *Wasil* (the One Who has Attained), and *Nujaba* (the Nobles), *Nukaba* (the Custodians), *Awtad* (the Pillars), *Qutb* (the Pole), *Qutbul-Aktab* (the Pole of Poles) and *Ghaws* (the Helper), *Emerald Hills of the Heart* discusses the relationship between God and His human creation with the most unique and sensitive aspects of this relationship, while at the same time it focuses on the identity of humans as of the best stature and the perfect pattern of creation by making use of the concept of the Perfect, Universal Human.

Another important attribute of *Emerald Hills of the Heart*, at least as important, if not more so, as the other attributes mentioned above, is that it presents the Islamic spiritual life that constitutes the core of Islam not as a theoretical subject but as lived by the Companions of the Prophet, may God be pleased with them all. It presents this life as a profound experience of the heart, mind, and body described and appointed by Islam. It also investigates how it has taken shape throughout history. *Emerald Hills of the Heart* bequeaths to future ages—a time in which perhaps apparently different realms of religion and reason, science, technology, rhetoric and welfare will, in cooperation, make unprecedented and inconceivable progress—the legacy of Sufism, with all its dimensions, or the spiritual life of Islam in its immense entirety as a safe and sound road that has been protected against all manners of deviation.

— Publisher

TALIB, MURID, SALIK, WASIL
(THE SEEKER, THE ONE WHO WILLS, THE INITIATE, THE ONE WHO HAS ATTAINED OR REACHED)

God is the ultimate goal and human beings are travelers on the road to Him; there are as many paths that lead toward God as there are breaths taken by living creatures. The facts that human beings are favored with the manifestations of the Divine Names, that the travelers are endowed with innate abilities, which are God's particular gifts to them, and that there is special attention and complimentary remarks directed towards them for services that will be rendered later are some of the signs that mark these paths. Without a doubt, the final goal is pleasing God or obtaining His approval and good pleasure; the greatest means of advancing towards this goal is the ability to recognize Him and to acquire knowledge of Him, as well as trying to inform others of Him. This is known as guidance. The differences in capacities and the great variety of human character and disposition have caused the creation of many efficient systems and methods of traveling toward Him. Those who travel toward Him according to these systems are able to make progress. Journeys can start at different points, but they continue through the same mansions or stations and culminate in some corner of the same "climate."

The final station for every traveler depends on the individual capacity to rise. Every traveler starts journeying at one particular station, quarter, seaport, airport or ramp. The starting point differs. However, the mansions that are passed, the areas that are reached, the horizons attained, the states experienced and the stations at which the travelers stop to rest are all in the same space, but adorned with different designs, like the slopes of Paradise, and tinted with different hues. The paths advance one within the other, or side by side, through hills and valleys, narrowing at some points and broadening at others; sometimes the way is rough and sometimes smooth. Travelers journey along them in different ways or with different styles. Many begin traveling these paths while many others are reaching the final point in their journey. Despite these apparent differences, the journey has the same essential character. A point which is considered to be the final point for one traveler may be the starting point for another. There are many others who suppose they are advancing, but who in fact are unable to cover the smallest distance, while the number of those who travel through the horizons that stretch beyond time and space and who are determined to rise higher and higher is not a few.

In fact, so long as there are hands that clasp the Unbreakable Rope and eyes and hearts fixed on the explicit, incontestable principles and judgments of the Qur'an and Sunna, then all paths lead to God and all travelers are travelers toward God, the Ultimate Truth. Different attitudes in journeying and different types of traveling arise from the comprehensiveness and practicability of the Religion; they are also the result of the breadth and tolerance that exist in fields open to deductive reasoning based on the basic principles, the various manifestations of Divine Names, and the variety of capacities. In any event, travelers advance toward God and it is for this reason that they are described as the travelers to the Ultimate Truth.

Rather than calling the travelers who advance via different paths by different names according to the profundity of their belief, the soundness of their Islamic understanding and approaches, the depth of their consciousness of God's omnipresence, the breadth and richness of their horizon of thought, the spaciousness of their conscience, the faultless operation of all of their internal and external senses, the optimum use of their mental and spiritual faculties, their capacity to rise while making their spiritual journey, their beginning their journey from the corporeal, created realm and continuing it based on the principles or commands of the spiritual realm and according to their sincerity, purity, resolution, steadfastness, and their faithfulness to the Ultimate Truth—rather than calling the travelers by different names according to these and certain other factors, I deem it more appropriate and practical to study them under the titles of "the seeker, the one who wills, the initiate, and the one who has attained or reached." While mentioning travelers to the Ultimate Truth by these titles, which are different from but at the same time interrelated to one another, we will sometimes use the term "one who has true knowledge of God" in place of the "one who wills," "the initiate," and "the one who has attained" on account of their horizon of knowledge of God.

Now let us study these titles one by one:

THE SEEKER

This is used for one who seeks, desires, and tries to obtain knowledge or some other blessing. As a term, the seeker denotes one who has newly begun their spiritual journey and who is trying to obtain primary information about knowledge, the knowledge of God, and truth; they are determined to attain that which they pursue. On account of being at the beginning of the journey, such a person may be deemed to be of little value or significance, but as all consequent advancements and blessings that come in parallel to these advancements depend on the demand and determination which the seeker has at the beginning, they are in fact a seed that is ready to sprout and flourish. In order to express the significance of such a seeking, the venerable Junayd al-Baghdadi says: "Whoever demands and seeks ultimately finds what he seeks."[1] This saying later came to be a popular adage.

---

1 Junayd al-Baghdadi (d. 910): One of the most famous early Sufis. He enjoyed great respect and was known as "The prince of the knowers of God." (Tr.)

The Sufis use the term "the seeker" to indicate one who has begun following a Sufi path under the leadership of a guide. However, when a seeker has fulfilled whatever is required for being equipped with will-power, they can sometimes achieve a sudden transformation from being a "seeker" to being "one who wills," and then advance as far as the horizon of "the initiate" through God's special favors and begin dreaming of reaching God. It sometimes occurs that a seeker remains restricted within the narrow horizon of seeking without being able to cover any distance despite their exhausting efforts to advance. We should also remember that there are conditions if a person is to be accepted as one who seeks. Every candidate is tested by a perfect guide in order to discover whether or not they have the character and manners that will enable them to make the journey. If they are found to be fit for the journey, they are then told, "Hold on to the hand of your guide and walk toward the Ultimate Truth." Being a seeker and a candidate for the rank of "one who wills," this traveler advances toward the realms that open unto their heart, and flies past the peaks that give way before their capacity. However, they should firmly clasp the hand to which they hold with the conviction that this hand is the means for them to reach their goal; they should fix their eyes on this "mirror" in their hands, in or through which they will be able to observe the manifestations of Divine Names, and they should avoid breaking it. They should also advance resolutely on the path they have taken, and remain devoted to it heart and soul. Muhammed Ali Hilmi Dede[2] puts forwards his ideas about the seeker as follows:

> One who seeks holds onto the hand of a guide,
> Submitting their soul and tongue to the Ultimate Truth.
> One who wills girds a sword around their waist,[3]
> Clinging firmly to the girdle of their guide.

---

2   Muhammed Hilmi Dede (1842–1907): One of the famous Baktashi Sufi masters of the 19th century. He lived in Istanbul. He has a *diwan*, a collection of poetry. (Tr.)

3   Saving one's hand, tongue and waist (private parts) from sinful acts is essential to Sufi way. "Girding a sword around one's waist" means that a seeker must strictly save their private parts from sinning. (Tr.)

If the seeker is one who truly seeks the light and gift of God, they should be steadfast in following the path without any deviance, always remaining turned toward Him in love, so that they can be regarded as truthful and faithful in their quest and favored with the regard and attention of He Who is the All-Besought One. Such a degree of dedication and devotion is what is required of one who wills and of one who is determined to give their free will its due.

THE ONE WHO WILLS OR THE WILLING ONE

According to the Sufis, the one who wills is one who after renouncing their personal desires and aims is attached to a guide in accordance with the religious rules and is under the guidance of this person for their spiritual training. This term is used to denote the dervishes who have not yet entered or who have been unable to enter the path of initiation; the first rank that will be attained by one who wills is annihilation in the guide.[4]

Muhyi'd-Din ibnu'l-'Arabi[5] defines the one who wills or the willing one as one who has renounced looking, seeing, and willing on their own account, but has rather turned wholly to God. This definition differs from other definitions. According to Ibnu'l-'Arabi, one who wills sees their free will as belonging to God and as a manifestation of His absolute Will, thus perceiving all other forms of will or volition as being relative or of a nominal existence and nature. If this consideration by Ibnu'l-'Arabi was a result of spiritual ecstasy, then no one has the right to criticize it. If this was not the case, then the scholars of essentials of religion would have had something to say about it. Even though those like the venera-

---

4 The one who wills or the willing one (*murid*) was discussed in the first volume of *Emerald Hills of the Heart* from another viewpoint together "the willed one (*murad*)."

5 Muhyi'd-Din ibnu'l-'Arabi (1165–1240): One of the greatest and most famous Sufi masters. His doctrine of the Transcendental Unity of Being, which most have mistaken for monism and pantheism, made him the target of unending polemics. He wrote many books, the most famous of which are *Fususu'l-Hikam* and *al-Futuhatu'l-Makkiyyah*. (Tr.)

ble Ibnu'l-'Arabi attribute free will to human beings, in theory, in the sense of inclination, they venerate those who have renounced their free will in the face of the Divine Will. The reason why there is a variety of approaches in such matters is partly due to differences in individual spiritual tastes, visions, experiences and states, as well as in temperaments and dispositions.

No matter who the person that one who wills is attached to, their real goal is God, the All-Besought One. However, all of those who will are not at the same level and may have different manners. There are some, known as "one who is absolutely sincere in their seeking," who never disagree with their guide and avoid manners that could be interpreted as opposing the guide. They do not search for evidence for the words and decrees of the guide in other places. There are others who, although they also follow the orders of their guide both apparently and at heart, and who do not feel the need to search for different ways or methods, are not as sensitive or as careful as the former in following or in attachment to the guide. Such people are called "one who wills figuratively." There are still yet others, if they can truly be regarded as being among those who will, who, even though they apparently comply with their guide, always breathe opposition to the guide in their absence and in their secret considerations; these latter think that it is of no harm to behave differently, zigzagging along the path. The Sufis use the term "deserter" to define such people.

The most important characteristics that are expected from one who wills are truthfulness, loyalty, trustworthiness, and straightforwardness. These are all the characteristics that belong to those who are stationed near to God. That is, among the attributes that one who wills should have are being true in words, actions, and thoughts, being mentioned as a trustworthy one in the heavens and on the earth, always giving the impression that one is utterly reliable, and being a person of steadfastness and resolution who gives their free will its due.

Despite being at the beginning of the journey, one who wills should always be respectful for the principles and criteria of the Shari'a, possessing the sensitivity of an initiate and observing the norms that are generally accepted by the Muslim community, thus avoiding religiously detestable things. If they happen to commit a repugnant act, even once, or fail to observe an accepted norm, the traveler should immediately hasten to the fountain of repentance, penitence, and contrition, with the thought of giving no respite to anything that is sinful or to any stain caused by having committed something that is displeasing to God. Without delay, they should be purified of the filth or viruses that can open up wounds in their heart and spirit.

In addition, such a traveler who is traveling the path toward the Ultimate Truth and seeking God's good pleasure should set their heart on the Ever-Besought One, thus cleansing their heart of attachment to wealth and earning, love of rank and position, desire for comfort, and interest in anything other than God. Moreover, they should regard being and not being, being favored with certain things and being deprived of them, gaining and losing, that which comes and that which does not come, that which remains and that which does not remain, and being accepted and being rejected all as equal. They should try to keep all these opposites equal in their world of the spirit.

As the final point for one who wills is annihilation in the Will of the Lord, complete obedience to the guide from the beginning is required. If one who wills is to continue to be favored with Divine regard, it is extraordinarily important that they obey the commandments given in accordance with the Shari'a without objection, fulfilling whatever they are advised to do and never neglecting the devotional recitations that they have undertaken to do regularly. These are preparatory and encouraging duties that are to be fulfilled for the full observance of the Qur'an and Sunna. It is clear that a traveler toward the Ultimate Truth who gives their free will its due in loyalty to their guide will be sensitive in the observation of the orders and prohibitions of the Ultimate Truth. However, they should avoid treating the guide, who is the mirror through which the Sun's rays—God's blessings—are reflected as if he were the Sun, that is, God, and thus considering the means to be the goal.

The attitude of the willing one or of one who wills in the face of God, their view of themselves and other people, and their approach to Divine gifts and bounties are also of great importance. First of all, they should see themselves as being inferior to all people and so that this view is not without support, they should always control, examine and criticize their faults. They should try to be aware of any faults or sins that catch their attention, as if they have newly committed them, busying themselves at every instant, every hour, and every day with their own purification, as well as completely abandoning finding fault with others. If the one who wills think that they have any merits, they should tremble in fear that these are present as a means for gradual perdition, as they have not been purified enough to be deserving of such blessings. They should not attribute to themselves any part of their praiseworthy activities, from their greatest services for the sake of God to their sincerest acts of worship, or from their most unbearable sufferings to their most difficult attempts of initiation; nor should they have any extraordinary expectations due to such actions. Even if they are favored with showers of gifts and blessings, they should worry that these may be coming as a test, saying like Muhammed Lutfi Efendi:

> That which I have—I am not worthy of it;
> This favor and grace—why have they been bestowed on me?[6]

The traveler should never think that they are worthy of any such attributes, and in order not to be ungrateful to God for them, they should feel gratitude in their heart and then utterly forget about them, without ever recollecting them. Otherwise, that which could

---

6   Muhammed Lutfi Efendi (1868–1956): One of the Sufi masters who lived in Erzurum. He has a *Divan* containing many beautiful, lyrical poems.

lead to triumph may end in a pit of loss and that which appears to be a gift may become the cause of frustration.

It cannot be thought that a willing one whose mind and heart are expectant of gifts and blessings, and whose feelings pursue unusual occurrences can have a sound relationship with God Almighty. How can it be thought that while they should actually be purifying their heart, the house of God, of anything other than God and always being concerned with God in their inner world, they are wasting their time on things that are outside the sphere of their duties and responsibilities, and thus constantly deviating towards disagreeable expectations?

One who wills has unshakable belief and confidence in the sufficiency of the Qur'an and the Sunna as the way of the Prophet, upon him be peace and blessings. Even though they are not at a level where they can use these two basic sources themselves, they should be deeply devoted to them with perfect regard, always preserving their conviction that they will be able to attain anything they seek via the Qur'an and Sunna, and realizing what a great blessing living a life in a continuous relationship with the Qur'an is; in this way they are able to remain distant from trivialities and fantasies that are an illusion of knowledge, but which are of no use for the mental or intellectual and spiritual life.

Every traveler toward the Ultimate Truth who has turned to God under the care of a guide and who is a hero of will-power and discipline must be careful in all matters, from their personal life to their relationships with their Lord, not allowing any contradiction to occur between their heart and their actions, but rather always acting in self-possession, and eating, drinking, sleeping, and talking little, restricting these activities to only what is necessary, regarding anything superfluous as waste. One who truly wills is steadfast in their opposition to their carnal soul and regards this opposition as a means of approaching nearer to God; at the same time such a person will consider following the carnal soul as a means of failure and loss. One who lives at peace with their carnal desires and fancies is not regarded as one who wills. For after having set out to attain God, if one replaces guidance with the pursuit of the realization of carnal desires, this means turning back upon the path on which they have embarked. This is considered to be desertion. One who wills should always be steadfast, waiting at the door to which they have turned and continuing on the road on which they have embarked, always displaying a spirit of deep loyalty. One who has been defeated in the test of willpower at the very outset can never be considered to be one of loyalty, faithfulness, trustworthiness, or straightforwardness. Nor is it possible for such a person to be able to read Divine Acts correctly, or to understand anything of the Divine Names, or to make sense of or comprehend the Divine Attributes. Every thought will be no more than a guess or a conjecture, and their every attitude and act will be deviant.

For the one who wills, for all travelers toward the Ultimate Truth, the following points are of the greatest importance:

A traveler should see themselves as nothing in the sense of positive values. They should use the initial gifts of God that arrive during the journey to attain the goal; this is the reason that they have been sent. Such a traveler should have no desire for anything worldly, rather they should be content with whatever they have and they should have utter confidence in God; they should be oblivious of themselves when it is time to distribute rewards in return for services rendered and try to find causes and agents other than themselves for the good results of their endeavors. Such a traveler should feel responsible for any failure or negative consequences without trying to blame others.

Other points which have almost the same importance are as follows:

- Piety and righteousness are provisions for the afterlife of the traveler. A person who intends to follow a spiritual path should always seek refuge in the "greenhouse" of piety, as decreed in the verse, *Take your provisions for the Hajj (for any long travel). In truth, the best provision is righteousness and piety, so be provided with righteousness and piety* (2:197).

- A traveler should be utterly sincere in whatever they do and say, as if they were presenting themselves for the inspection of God Almighty, the holy Prophet, upon him be peace and blessings, and other pure spiritual beings.

- As decreed in *Always be in the company of the truthful and loyal* (9:119), the traveler should choose their friends and comrades from among the people of loyalty and trustworthiness. This is extraordinarily important for a safe journey. Being near to those who are near to God and keeping aloof from selfish, arrogant ones—provided that one refrains from causing the formation of conflicting groups in society—is important, particularly for the principle of preventing harm and evil.

- Respect for the elderly, pity, care and concern for children, and compassion for all human beings are requirements for all Muslims and therefore are required when following a spiritual path.

- A traveler should try to remain pure in the face of God, preserving their primordial nature that was bestowed on them in its purest form; if they should happen to lapse, they should turn to God in their heart, criticize themselves, and be purified with repentance; they should then ask for forgiveness, cutting off at the root the tendencies to evil in their soul, and always be alert to any further possible evil acts or lapses.

- Ostentation, hypocrisy, affectation, and love of fame are regarded as being among the most lethal viruses from which a traveler must protect themselves. If a heart cannot remain distant from these, its balance is disturbed. One cannot search for any Divine manifestation with such a heart, and the bosom in which it nestles cannot be a pavilion for any Divine manifestations that might come.

- The heart is a house of God. It must be kept pure for its Owner's sake so that a traveler does not darken the most vital dimension of their being or cause any eclipses in their spiritual life while possessing such a source of light.

A traveler with such important responsibilities should be under the leadership of a guide on this path, which is full of risks, while it is also on this path that travelers may be favored with as many precious gifts and blessings as are required for gaining eternal happiness. This leadership is important for both the safety of the journey and advancement without deviation. However, a guide is only a mirror and one who shows the way. Therefore, they should never be regarded as the actual leader that enables the traveler to advance or the source of the gifts and blessings that come during the journey. It is a deviance of creed to consider the guide as a supreme being or one having superhuman attributes, or the source of all gifts and blessings. Such a deviance also blocks the breezes of favor that originate from the Genuine Source. This does not mean that a traveler should not pay due respect to the guide; the guide is a mirror that reflects these gifts and blessings. The breezes of favor that come from the Realm of Mercy reach us in the atmosphere of the guide; Divine gifts and blessings are reflected on our spirits by means of the guide as a mirror and the guide functions as a veil before God's Grandeur and Dignity. They serve their followers sometimes as light, sometimes as air, sometimes as water, and sometimes as food, functioning as a means for their rising. Let us finish this discussion with the following stanza from Anwari:[7]

> The meaning of "You will never be able to see Me":
> I could not understand it without being
> "Mount Sinai" in tearful love.

---

[7] Awhadu'd-Din 'Ali Anwari is a famous poet who lived in the 12th century in Iran and Afghanistan. Besides poetry, he was adept in logic, music, theology, mathematics, and astrology. His *Diwan*, a collection of his poems, consists of a series of long poems, and a number of simpler lyrics. (Tr.)

The mystery of the truth of the cloak that covers
the Prophet's Family.[8]
I could not understand this without being happy
when meeting a guide.

Some Sufi scholars call one who has just set off on the spiritual path "the one who wills or the willing one," and they refer to
the one who has reached the end of the path as "the one who is
willed or the willed one." They see the former as a hero of suffering and hardship, and the latter as a hero of Divine grace who is favored with attraction and being attracted toward God. In my opinion, a traveler who has just set off on the path is the one who is on
the way to being one who wills, while when they approach the horizon of the initiate in endeavors to reach God they have reached
the final point of being one who wills.

> O God! Guide us to the Straight Path. Shower on us from Your
> supreme Grace and pour on us from Your Mercy, O the All-
> Merciful, the All-Compassionate. Bestow blessings and peace on
> the one whom You sent as mercy for all the worlds, and on his
> Family and Companions, pure and clean.

---

8   Once the Prophet, upon him be peace and blessings, covered his daughter Fatima,
    her husband 'Ali and their sons Hasan and Husayn with a cloak, and said: "This is
    my Family." So they have also been called the People of the Cloak. (Tr.)

THE INITIATE FROM A DIFFERENT PERSPECTIVE

An initiate is one who follows a way. In Sufi terminology, the word "initiate" denotes one who walks toward God with a certain discipline in order to please Him, thus neutralizing the tendencies in their nature that lead them away from God, or trying to eliminate the distance between them and God. There are two kinds of initiate:

- The first is the initiate who, without having to fulfill the requirements of following a spiritual path, passing through certain periods of suffering, or staying with a guide for a fixed amount of time, can pass through all states and stations in one attempt and reach the highest point destined for him by being attracted by God Himself. This is the initiate who is attracted or feels attraction toward God.
- The striving initiate, who follows a spiritual path toward God either within their inner world or through the outer world in conformity with the requirements of the journey.

However, despite these two basic categories, there can be interconnections and transitions between these two different methods of initiation, or different states or conditions may occur in the way of attraction. For example, one who feels attracted toward God may lose this feeling at one point, only to regain it later without having had to enter a path. Or an attracted initiate who loses the feeling of attraction may feel it again after they have begun to follow a path. Referring such matters to the heroes of Sufi practice, I would like to discuss the initiate who walks toward the Ultimate Truth within their inner world or through the outer world.

The first step in initiation is intention. Intention is the beginning of every action; it is both the beginning and the foundation stone of initiation, without which any action is devoid of spirit and thus walking toward God is impossible. If a pure intention is strengthened through dependence on God's help and sharpened through resolution and steadfastness, then an initiate can succeed in every attempt with God's permission and will be able to overcome every obstacle; indeed, one day they will reach the final point according to their capacity. However, it is clear that there is need for a perfect guide along this path, as it is one which extends through many mansions, stations, and deep valleys; sometimes it is a highway and sometimes a trail. Along this road many difficulties await the traveler. For this reason, woe betide the initiate whose guide or master is a pretender or an insufficient one who claims to be a guide. The following couplet by Niyazi-i Mısri[9] expresses this beautifully:

> Let not any guide lead you, for he may make it
> too difficult to proceed;
> It is very easy for one whose guide is perfect
> to advance along this path.

Initiation is another way of discovering and experiencing the truths of belief and being a Muslim in accordance with their true nature. The initiate recognized them partly while they were a seeker, and became familiar with some of their manifestations at different degrees while they were the one who wills. Peace of heart, the elixir of which many talk without knowing its true essence, is drunk by the glassful during initiation. Reverent awe of God can also be experienced in this way as well. In addition, that which is experienced becomes the depth of human nature at different de-

---

9   Mehmet Niyazi-i Misri (1617–1694). He was born in Malatya, Turkey, and died in the island of Limni in the Agean Sea. He was a Sufi *shaykh*, poet, and scholar. *Ilmihal-i Tariqat* ("The Principles of the Sufi Way"), *Mawadiul-'Irfan* ("The Tables of Esoteric Knowledge"), and *Tevhid Risalesi* (A Treatise of God's Oneness") are among his most famous works. (Tr.)

grees; in other words, belief, which was obtained on the horizon of theory, is grasped and experienced on the horizon of practice along such a journey made in the atmosphere of the heart and spirit. Having risen to certain heights through constant travel along this path and having been matured in virtues and praiseworthy characteristics, the initiate follows a line along which spirit beings move and reach scenes that lie beyond the horizon. The initiate elevates their theoretical knowledge to the level of experienced knowledge of God and is filled with lights both inwardly and outwardly, pitching their pavilion of glory at the station that is best suited for their state and stance.

It sometimes happens that a traveler with an illuminated heart and this degree of knowledge of God finds themselves in different states and manners, and they are enveloped by the colors that belong to the realms beyond; thus the ways to spiritual pleasures and vision are opened to the traveler. Nevertheless, there are many who are deceived by these occurrences and remain at a halfway point. Only the alert travelers overcome this stagnation by God's leave and continue their journey. Such occurrences are neither the aim of worship nor the goal of initiation. One who perceives these as the goal cannot know the True Goal, and one who aims at these cannot obtain anything other than weariness. For this reason, the heroes of knowledge of God try to remain distant from such things, even in their dreams, fearful that such manifestations occurring without demand might lead them to perdition; at the same time they respond to the Divine gifts of which they are aware in their conscience with gratitude. If these are offerings from the All-Merciful and favors from God Almighty that increase the initiate's zeal and yearning—it is not possible for us to say that they are truly thus or not – the traveler should think that they are being faced by a new shower of bounties and thus be full of thanks and enthusiasm, changing the acts of formal worship into acts of deep devotion, enriching their life with the depths of the night (spending some of their night in worship), and all their acts should demonstrate that they are a careful servant of God —they should do all of this, but never feel proud of these, never pursue fame or feel superior to others, as this will darken the manifestations that come in waves from the Realm of Mercy with the soot and rust of selfishness, arrogance, ostentation and the desire for fame. The traveler should realize that all these gifts and favors come due to their awareness of their innate impotence, poverty, and neediness before God, and thus they should not appropriate them. They should concentrate on the Real Source of these bounties and be fearful that they may be a test; thus, they should always seek refuge in God, and consider that such bounties may be a means of encouragement to further and better worship. As a result, the traveler should try to worship more consciously and in constant awareness of God's omnipresence. They should worship God with the awareness that all they do in the name of worship is nothing but an insignificant response to the bounties that they have received in advance.

This is what is expected from a traveler to the Ultimate Truth who always controls, criticizes, and supervises themselves. Such a traveler knows their place and always feels and voices their inability to know, worship, mention, and thank God as He should be worshipped, known, mentioned, and thanked, saying:

> All-Glorified are You, We have not been able to worship You
> as worshipping You requires, O the All-Worshipped.
> All-Glorified are You, We have not been able to know You
> as knowing You requires, O the All-Known.
> All-Glorified are You, we have not been able to mention You
> as mentioning You requires, O the All-Mentioned.
> All-Glorified are You, we have not been able to thank You
> as thanking You requires, O the All-Thanked.

Moreover, such a traveler always feels agony, shame, fear, and anxiety because of the faults they have or may have made and the sins they have or may have committed knowingly or unknowingly, as well as their manners and behavior that are displeasing to God. They are in a state in which they are about to undergo the questioning of the grave at that moment; they are afraid as if their actions were about to be weighed in the Hereafter. The traveler seeks refuge in God with utmost repentance and dies once again in respect of their carnal desires, feeling a new revival in consideration of their deeper attachment to God, as if they have heard the sound of the Trumpet (which is to be blown for the resurrection of the dead), trying to build a new world in the horizon of their heart and spirit. This should be a world where the traveler will constantly think of God, mention God, turn to God, converse with God, and receive breezes of revival from the realms beyond. They will always be in the company of their guide, fully submitted to the spirit of the master of creation, Prophet Muhammad, upon him be peace and blessings, in their royal pavilion pitched in closeness to God. This is a station where existence ends in non-existence and non-existence will take on a new, ever-fresh existence. The clocks always indicate mid-day at this station, the east and west are one within another, daytime and night are fused together, and the physical and metaphysical cannot be distinguished. Space is replaced by absence of space, and time is replaced with timelessness. The inhabitants of this station comprehend that everything belongs to and is originated by God and that they are on the way of return to Him, ultimately to end in Him. Breasts begin to burn with the fire of feeling His nearness and with the awareness that meeting with Him is almost at hand. Lips begin to murmur the things expected to come from Him, the things of which they are aware and partially experience; they remain waiting in great hope. As if overcoming whatever should be overcome, the heart says: "My God! I ask for the pleasure of looking toward Your Face, and a yearning to meet with You!" They are in a turmoil due to the expectation of the vision of His perfectly beautiful Face, the source of all beauties, and the desire to meet with Him. With an inextinguishable love and inexhaustible zeal, the heart utters: "I ask for the highest of grades and the greatest of goals!" and begins to wait for the realization of the expected meeting. Who knows how many times a day such a person imagines themselves to be seated at the table of this meeting, taking sips of the water of the Divine regard and consideration, voicing their yearning, saying:

> O cupbearer, offer the wine: it is time to break the fast;
> Improve this ruin: it is time to display the favors.
>
> Muhammed Lutfi

Then, sighing that the coming of the time to "break the fast" is dependent on God, the travelers pull themselves together.

Even though they are few in number at present, the initiates are the means of pride for the inhabitants of the heavens; these inhabitants watch them and take pride in their nearness to God. As stated in the verse, *And it has never been the way of your Lord to destroy the townships unjustly while their people were righteous, dedicated to continuous self-reform and setting things right in the society* (11:117), the initiates are the resilient barricade against possible calamities and the means of security.

Whether they be among those who are attracted by God Himself, or those who follow a spiritual path, or those who base their journey on the acceptance of human innate impotence and poverty, an initiate is one whose eyes are fixed on the door of the Ultimate Truth, who advances in adherence to the Prophetic way, trying to be equipped with knowledge of God and careful in their relations with their Lord; such a person always acts in awareness of God's omnipresence. It is as if they are about to meet with Him; in their every state, they feel a yearning to meet with God at the same time as being in awe of God and fluctuating between hope and fear. Sometimes they feel that they are on the horizon of certainty of observation, perceiving what seems to be imperceptible according to the profundity of their knowledge of God, attaining points that seem to be unattainable and observing what seems beyond the limits of observation, beyond all terms of quality and quantity. At other times they are lost in more comprehensive and profound visions, breathing the light-diffusing words, *God it is Who is the All-Known; God it is Who is the All-Besought, God it is Who is the All-Worshipped*! They constantly mention God, fixing their eyes on Him and worshipping Him exclusively. Haqani[10] describes an initiate of this quality in the following couplet:

> What is befitting for an initiate—a follower of the path,
> Is that he should proclaim: "We worship none but Him alone."

An initiate may encounter certain surprises during their journey, even though they expect nothing; they are transformed from one state into another and they may hear voices from the realms beyond, receiving compliments from spirit beings. However, their duty is to advance toward God without ceasing; they travel from God toward God, from themselves toward Him. They grasp hold of one Divine Name and walk toward the next; while flying in the atmosphere of one Name, they observe different beauties as manifestations of another.

It sometimes happens that an initiate begins traveling from God toward God on the wings of attraction and being attracted, while at other times they travel from the horizon of His company into the depths of their own nature. Through such descents and ascensions they make journeys like "journeying in" and "with or in the company of God," in addition to making other "journeys" toward further points through doing good, righteous deeds, the purification of the soul, refinement of the heart, and asceticism. However, some initiates are always with God, beginning from Him and reaching the final point allowed by their capacities in His company. Some initiates are always turned to God in their hearts, feeling that He is nearer to them than their own selves. But they feel that they are caught up in a net that holds them at a certain

---

10　Haqani, Afzalu'd-Din Ibrahim Badil ibn Ali (1126–1199) is one of the greatest poets in Persian literature. He was from Azerbaijan. He lived a hard life amidst the political turmoil of the time. His poems of praise for the Messenger are very beautiful. His *Diwan* and *Tuhfatul-Iraqany* are famous. (Tr.)

distance from Him and they are continuously trying to cover this distance. Some others are near to God and aware of this nearness; they do their utmost to preserve this favor of being near. If a traveler bases their initiation or journey on constant companionship of God, no matter in what way this has been adopted, God is their eyes with which they see, their ears with which they hear, and the source of all their outer and inner sensations. So long as an initiate at this degree of spiritual existence continues in turning to Him, is able to purify their heart of any relationship with anything other than God, and can make this state a dimension of their nature, then all the carnal and material things in their nature melt away in the face of the dominion of their spirituality. As a consequence, the initiate who has nearly attained their destination achieves a "magical" state in which it is as if they have neither corporeality nor substance. Their nature displays the characteristic of being an immaterial being that has nothing to do with soil, water, air, or any other material object. They are in the heavens at the same time as they are on the earth; they are walking through tomorrow while living today. Even though they seem to be condemned to remaining distant from God with their corporeal being, they continuously breathe nearness in the spirit; even though they appear to be fixed in a narrow place in space with their transient body, with their eternally-young, spiritual being, they are a guest in many places at the same instant, giving a hand to many needy ones on the land like Khadr,[11] and busy themselves with saving many others from drowning in the sea like Ilyas.[12]

---

11 (al-)Khadr is he with whom the Qur'an recounts (18: 60–82) the Prophet Moses, upon him be peace, made a journey to learn something of the spiritual realm of existence and the nature of God's acts in it. It is controversial whether he was a Prophet or merely a saint with a special mission. It is believed that he enjoys the degree of life where one feels no need for the necessities of normal human life, and may come to the aid of those who are in dire need on land. (Tr.)

12 Ilyas is one of the great Prophets mentioned in the Qur'an. Some scholars identify with Elijah, whom God sent to the Children of Israel during the reign of King Ahab in Israel, who was notorious for his injustices. He struggled against deviances in belief, immoralities, and injustices. It is believed that like Khadr, he enjoys the

So long as an initiate preserves this degree of spirituality, the showers of Divine attention continue to increase and this elevated state becomes their nature. Such an initiate is considered to have a station or rank, even if it be in a relative sense. Whatever they see is regarded as being the truth. Whatever they hear and feel is always of the same color and design. Their speeches manifest Divine inspirations and are blessed with the value of "pearl and coral," and thus have great effects on the audience. For they are initiates who are honored with established nearness to God, and whose knowledge is from God; they are those who see, hear and speak wholly dependent on God's permission, thus they evaluate everything according to the knowledge that emanates to them from His Presence.

Whether the initiate travels on the way of ascension from God toward God on the wings of attraction and the feeling of being attracted or on the way of descent from God toward their own essence; or whether they are trying to cover their distance from God, even though they are aware of God's nearness, or to preserve their nearness to God that they are aware of in themselves, the initiate is favored with Divine attraction and the capacity to cover all distances. Whether or not they experience any of the states through which they pass during their journey, the initiate reaches their destination with a single bound through Divine attraction and pitches their pavilion in the very center of the station. As for the heroes of effort and endeavor, they continually advance during their journey, covering distances and passing through many states. Covering the distances at a run, enduring the hardships and troubles that they encounter, and increasing in the knowledge of God that they acquire during their journey, they advance toward their final point, destined by their capacities, as if climbing stairs. They can also meet with God to some degree, but this cannot be compared with the favor that emanates to initiates from God's special treasury.

---

degree of life where one feels no need for the necessities of normal human life, and may come to the aid of those who are in dire need in the sea. (Tr.)

In short: the start of initiation is the perception and realization of the truth of Islam or being Muslim; the end is full awareness of God's omnipresence, or in other words, living a life as if always seeing God. The initiation is also the title of belief that has the degree of full conviction and full submission to God throughout an entire life, and an excellence or virtue in the meaning of worshipping God as if seeing Him or being aware that He always sees us. As for meeting with God, which is the final point or destination of the journey or travel, it is what the sensation or experience that transcends all time and space is called.

> O God! Guide us to the Straight Path. Shower blessings on us from Your supreme Grace, and let Your Mercy pour down on us, O the All-Merciful, the All-Compassionate! Bestow blessings and peace on the one whom You sent as a mercy for all the worlds, and on his Family and Companions, pure and clean.

WASIL

(ONE WHO HAS ATTAINED OR REACHED)[13]

Literally meaning one who has reached the final point in a journey or who has met with the one or the thing that one intends to reach, *wasil*, in Sufi terminology, denotes one who, having been saved from all the veils of corporeality and carnality one after the other, and who has covered all the distances that originate from themselves, has reached the final point of their journey, where they feel and experience the company of God Almighty, Who is the nearest of all to everyone and every thing.

Surmounting all the veils of corporeality that surround a human being, one within the other, and reaching the horizon of experiencing God's company is possible sometimes by God's special help and attention, sometimes by special knowledge of God, sometimes by the serious endeavors and efforts made during a spiritual journey, sometimes by following a path in which we admit our innate impotence and poverty, as well as our enthusiasm and thankfulness, and sometimes by extraordinary Divine attraction. All of these means of reaching the final point of the spiritual journey are the manifestations of God's grace on different wavelengths. Without His grace and special attention, a traveler can neither be saved from the veils of corporeality and carnality nor cover the distances

---

13 Meeting with God and *Wasil* (the one who has attained or reached) have been described in the third volume of *Emerald Hills of the Heart – Key Concepts in the Practice of Sufism*, pp. 16–24. Here it is described together with "the one who wills" and "the initiate" on account of the final gifts that come in return for meeting with God or reaching the end of the journey, and the self-possession that is required in return for these gifts.

that originate from themselves to reach the intended horizon. God is the One Who is the nearest of all to everyone and every thing, and it is He Who also brings those who strive to reach Him for His sake closer to Himself. Unless God brings us near, no one can feel the delight, which is called meeting, nor can they experience His company.

> When God manifests His grace, He makes everything easy;
> He creates the means of doing it and bestows it instantly.
>
> Anonymous

Common people can experience such a meeting or its shadow when they go to the other world with belief. However, there may be among them those who are drawn to the realms beyond through an extraordinary grace and who are favored with special compliments.

As for the elect who are God's noble, greatly favored servants, they traverse the distances that originate in themselves while they are still in the world, feeling as if they are experiencing the truth of *We are nearer to him than his jugular vein* (50:16) from the horizon of the observation of the heart and spirit, each according to the degree of their conviction and knowledge of God and their place in God's sight. They breathe God's company in their inner world.

There are others who are more advanced than the elect. They are the heroes of special favor and attention. They observe such things from the horizon of the spiritual intellect and through the mysterious windows of "secret," beyond all modalities of quality and quantity and beyond the limits of time and space, that they have neither been seen by other eyes nor heard by other ears nor conceived of by other minds. We can describe these as the heroes who state: "If the veils between were removed, my certainty would not increase."

If these heroes have reached that highest rank by following a spiritual path, then they are journeying "in God." They rotate like satellites around the lights and mysteries of the Ultimate Truth, increasing more and more in profundity with every attempt they make, and even though they have realized the meeting with the One of all eternity, their journey toward Him is never-ending. They constantly pursue observations beyond "certainty of knowledge," continuously seek visions that lie beyond "certainty of observation," and experience intoxicating pleasures through the manifestations reflected in their world of spirit that emanate from the door that has been partially opened on "certainty of experience."

This peak of spirituality is where every hero of truth comes to see, know, hear, and experience the mysteries that belong to the realms beyond, and clearly discovers and witnesses the original essence and nature of everything animate or inanimate and their relationship with the Creator; in addition they are aware of the fact that everything belongs to Him, subsists with Him, and is bound to return and on the way of returning to Him. Those who are able to observe existence from this peak clearly see what is light and what is of light, what is separation and what is union, what is the pang of separation and what is the delight of reunion, what is transient and who is eternal, what is bound to decay and what is permanent. They confirm the truth of their theoretical knowledge on the basis of witnessing, observation, and experience.

Since this peak is also the horizon from which the Prophets, pure, saintly scholars, and saints observe and monitor the realms beyond, it is such an awe-inspiring and delightful area of special study for the heroes of meeting with God that it is impossibly difficult for there to be another Divine favor in the world equal to it. Reaching this point is a supreme attainment and rank; the favors that emanate from there are many and multifarious, and the point itself is where the world and the Hereafter are observed together. However, the hero of meeting who is distinguished with such degree of Divine attention and favors is and should be extremely reticent about the favors with which they have been honored, and is absolutely modest. They try to conceal their relationship with God even from their own eyes. Just as Divine Grandeur and Dignity require that there to be veils before the acts of God's Power in the corporeal world, so too, the one who has reached the final point of journeying toward God and has been established there should not reveal the gifts that emanate at the peak of meeting with God. Even while they continue their relationships with the realms beyond the peak, they should frequently look down at the first step of the stairway which they have used to rise to that level and sigh in the consideration of: "We have not been able to know You as knowing You requires, O the All-Known!", thus admitting their inability to worship God as the duty of worshipping God requires. As a result of this realization, they say: "We have not been able to worship You as worshipping You requires, O the All-Worshipped!" Thinking: "Why am I blessed with these Divine compliments and consideration even though I have never done anything to deserve them?", the traveler should consider that whatever favor they have been honored with is purely a Divine gift.

If one with true knowledge of God, whose eyes are fixed only on the lights and mysteries beyond the Names and Attributes, attempts to reveal the Divine mysteries that they have perceived, they will not only be stunted, but will also cause shock and astonishment in the spirits of others. For this reason, such a person keeps their love and yearning buried in their bosom as something secret that has been entrusted to them, and they never reveal, nor are they permitted to reveal, the mysteries that belong to the realms beyond to those who have not yet been able to surpass themselves.

In fact, there are many who talk about these mysteries, but I think what they relate as mysteries must be their dreams or daydreams. All of those who talk about meeting with God are not ones who have reached the final point of spiritual journeying to meet with Him, just as everyone who follows a spiritual path is not one with true knowledge of God. One who has true knowledge of God is a hero confirmed by Divine grace, and is one who clearly observes the realms of Divine Names and Attributes and reads and comments what they observe correctly and without throwing others into confusion. This hero's perception and awareness of the meanings that radiate from the corporeal or physical realm is called "knowledge which is true," while their observation of the lights and mysteries that belong to the realms beyond and further than beyond is termed as "knowledge of the truth." The Absolute Pourer of blessings causes this hero of spiritual knowledge to be aware of the mystery of His Glory beyond description, perception, and comparison, making this person happy and rejoiced with His special attention and consideration. Even though the mind cannot comprehend the true nature and occurrence of this mysterious favor, the conscious nature or conscience feels this trust with its particular capacity in waves of awe and amazement. The tongue prefers silence and the spirit falls silent in contemplation.

"Knowledge of God's Acts" is a Divine gift that may be sent to every initiate; "knowledge of Divine Attributes and Essential Qualities or Characteristics" is a heavenly offering to the elect with a special capacity. "Knowledge of the truth" is a Divine favor and award for the most elect who have attained the level of developing their angelic aspect. Let those who are incapable of understanding continue not to understand, and those who are reluctant to accept insist on non-acceptance, those who are distinguished with knowledge of God constantly observe these mysteries and lights with the eyes of their souls and live in ecstasy.

> In the eyes of the soul of those with knowledge of God
> there exists the light of spiritual knowledge;
> God's help comes to them with
> the attainment of the mystery of this knowledge.
>
> Muhammed Lutfi

As was summarized before (in the 2nd volume of *Emerald Hills of the Heart*) under the title of *Ma'rifa* (Knowledge of God), the attainments on the path toward knowledge of God are a mount, while those who have attained this knowledge are the rider, and their knowledge is their capital. For this reason, those who are devoid of this knowledge cannot traverse the distance from Him nor reach the point of meeting with Him, while a hero of this knowledge and meeting never thinks of turning back or being the lover of others. Why and how can such a person think such a thing when, in the words of Yunus,[14] they have found the choicest honey or the true source of all honey and have been nearly saved from the love of even their own soul. They have attained "the manifest conquest" or even "the absolute conquest," which means being on the horizon of the manifestation of Divine Essence. Some of those who have been honored with this attainment at times live in such absorption and intoxication, like a happy one in whom the Lights of God are reflected, that they are aware of no one other than God, including themselves.

It should also be pointed out that there are so many degrees and levels of feeling and experience in this extraordinary attainment called "meeting with God" that none of the beloved servants of God who travel along the same route or axis can completely perceive the nature of another's meeting with Him. Just as saints can know the ranks of each other only if God allows them to, the heroes of meeting being able to perceive the nature of others' meeting with Him is also dependent on Divine inspiration. Unless God makes it known, no one can know what or where somebody is; students or initiates cannot know the mysteries of the guide's or master's meeting with God, and the master or guide cannot discover how a perfect student or an initiate with knowledge of God travels toward and realizes meeting with Him. It is the Creator Who knows everything, and others can know only to the extent that God allows them to know.

For this reason, as it was also the case with some of the Companions of the Prophet, upon him be peace and blessings,

---

14 Yunus Emre (1240–1320). One of the most famous Sufi folk poets who have made a great impact on the Muslim-Turkish culture. His philosophy, metaphysics and humanism have been examined in various symposiums and conferences on a regular basis both in Turkey and abroad. (Tr.)

since many perfect human beings, at least many travelers toward God who are candidates for perfection—even though they are favored with knowledge of God and meeting with God—cannot or are not allowed to know the horizon of those who have close relationships with God or the peak where they stand, they may not accept others of the same degree of nearness to God as them, even though the latter are pure, saintly scholars who are heirs to the mission of the Prophets; they may even go so far as to disparage them. This standpoint may sometimes be a risky trial for the travelers on the path toward God. Although, provided they keep silent about others and purify their hearts of bad moral qualities, they are candidates to be the doves of the heaven of sainthood, they suffer losses on the way to earning, either due to their biased love of their own ways or their hostility toward others or envy of God's favors on others, and cause the people of heresy and unbelief to rejoice by taking up a stance against God's close friends. Another cause of loss is that one sees oneself and their group as being great and qualified to guide others, while perceiving of others as insignificant and in need of guidance. There are as many paths toward God as the breaths of creatures and it is possible for everyone who travels toward Him sincerely to attain a certain degree of nearness to God and to realize some sort of meeting with Him. It is not vanity, self-esteem, self-assertion, or pretension, but modesty, self-denial, and mortification that are fundamentally important in traveling toward God. No one knows how many people who have been paid no importance by others have reached the Ultimate Truth, while many others who are self-esteemed and hold a position in people's eyes have remained at the half-way point.

I think it is fitting to put an end to this parenthetical discussion with the following stanza by Ibrahim Haqqi of Erzurum:[15]

---

15 Ibrahim Haqqi of Erzurum (1703–1780) was one of the most outstanding figures in the Ottoman Turkey of the 18th century. He lived in Erzurum and Siirt in the Eastern Turkey. He was a prolific, encyclopedic Sufi guide and writer,

Haqqi, come and do not reveal your secret,
If you intend to become matured on this path.
Do not look down on the people who are ruined in appearance,
There are ruins that hold secret treasures.

* * *

It is primarily dependent on God's grace and help – may God never leave us deprived of His grace and help – and secondarily on the endeavor (*himma*) of the servant that the one who wills or the willing one can desire God, and that an initiate can travel toward Him in accordance with the rules of travel, and that one who has reached the end of the path to reach Him can traverse the distances originating in themselves, and that all these Divine favors and blessings continue. Endeavor is an important provision for one who has reached the end of the path and God's intimacy or special nearness and treatment is a special favor of Divine companionship for such a hero.

When used concerning the servants of God, the term *himma* (endeavor) means trying, self-exertion, making an effort, resolution, starting an approvable task with sincere intention and feeling the excitement of responsibility with all the strength of the heart; when this term is used to refer to God, it denotes His response to all these activities (with special succor and reward).

Endeavor is an important dynamic for the traveler to the Ultimate Truth. The peaks that seem to be insurmountable are usually surmounted through endeavor, and it is also through endeavor that the steps along the stairway toward God and the pleasures and states of meeting with Him are determined. However, the travelers, the heroes of endeavor, are different from one another. A traveler who is always alert, in continuous pursuit of the realization of a goal with all their outer and inner senses, and always dreams of meeting with God with their eyes fixed on the door—such a travel-

---

who wrote in many subjects such as Theology, Morality, Mathematics, Astronomy, and Medicine. His *Ma'rifatname* ("The Book of Knowledge") is very famous and still being widely read. (Tr.)

er adopts a posture in the location where they are particular to themselves. While the posture of those who are trying to fulfill the Divine purpose of their creation in all their acts by carrying out what is necessary with their free will, is one of standing in perfect respect at the door of God. The worshipful attitude of another, of the hero of meeting with God, the one who has assigned all their endeavors, every day, hour, minute, and second of their life to earning God's approval and good pleasure, and who is distant from all considerations of state and station, who always thinks of and mentions God alone, and turns to God on the way of knowing Him with perfect certainty, and who is forgetful of their own desires, seeking God alone, preferring a single instant spent in His sacred company to any other achievement – this worshipful attitude of such a hero of meeting is completely different.

In fact, being freed from all other physical and spiritual relationships, our turning to the Ultimate Truth with a feeling of great need and melting away in Him is God's right on us and our duty toward Him. A human being has a single heart that can bear the love of a single beloved. For this reason, we should assign this Divine intellect of ours to His love alone, closing all doors on everything but Him, and fixing our eyes on Him in utter oblivion of even ourselves, with a yearning to meet the All-Loved and Besought One. A person is valuable to the extent of their endeavors. Thus, one who has reached God after a faultless journey is also a hero of endeavor.

The author of *al-Lujja*[16] expresses this heroism as follows:

> If you want to fly upwards, unfold your wings of endeavor,
> For what is primarily required for flying are wings.

16　The author of *al-Lujja* is Mawlana Nuru'd-Din 'Abdu'r-Rahman ibn Ahmad al-Jami' (1414–1492). He is commonly called the last great classical poet of Persia, and was a saint. He composed numerous lyrics and idylls, as well as many works in prose. His *Salaman wu Absal* is an allegory of profane and sacred love. Some of his other works include *Haft Awrang, Tuhfatu'l-Ahrar, Layla wu Majnun, Fatihatu'sh-Shabab, Lawa'ih, ad-Durrah*. (Tr.)

Those who have kept their wings of endeavor stretched out have, by God's leave, neither remained half-way nor fallen prey to wild beasts.

Some have interpreted endeavor as purifying one's bodily life from attachment to anything worldly, one's spiritual life from the pursuit of spiritual pleasures, and one's heart from consideration of Paradise and its pleasures, thus being turned to the Truly Worshipped, Deservedly Besought One with all of one's senses and faculties. I think they refer to the whole-hearted devotion which is mentioned in the verse, *And keep in remembrance the Name of your Lord (and mention It in your Prayer), and devote yourself to Him whole-heartedly* (73:8), which expresses a special attitude of nearness to God for those who have a special relationship with Him, and is a call to a different, special meeting with Him. Prophet Muhammad, upon him be peace and blessings, was the unequalled hero of such whole-hearted devotion and the foremost addressee of such a call. He covered his distance from God and was the nearest of all to Him. Despite this, Prophet Muhammad never slackened in his endeavors and used to make extraordinary efforts to be able to remain turned to Him and to meet with Him. He was in continuous pursuit of "what is more and further," for he was the guide of all initiates, and the leader of all who reached and would reach Him. For this reason, he guided everybody to the path of becoming close to God and instructed them in the manners that were to be assumed for His company and His special nearness. This path requires endeavor, and that horizon wants freedom from any inclination to anything else but Him. How beautifully the author of *al-Minhaj* speaks:

> You will never be able to have special nearness
> to Him in His private "lodge,"
> Until you are completely freed from inclination
> to any other but Him.

It is a requirement of courtesy to take off one's worn-out clothes so that one can don the garment of satin offered by the Sultan. Being a most important aspect of human nature, the heart is a house of God in the sense that it is where His special attention and favors are manifested. Unless it is purified of any trace that belongs to others than Him, the Sultan will not turn to it with favor, and without this, meeting with Him is not possible. Everyone who has arrived at the end of the path and whom the Ultimate Truth has honored by making them aware of His nearness experiences some degree of meeting, according to their capacity and the breadth and brightness of their mirror of spirit. The meeting of some is crowned with God's special nearness and relationship and the one who has attained this degree of meeting is regarded as an "intimate one." Literally meaning a close, bosom friend, this term in the terminology of some Sufi masters denotes one who feels togetherness with God at heart and in spirit to the extent that they only think of Him, with everybody else having completely disappeared from sight and being removed from the heart. This is companionship with God that is experienced beyond time and space and beyond all modalities of quality and quantity.

Some heroes of meeting voice this honor of special nearness by continuously mentioning God with His Acts, Names, and Attributes. This favor is called "intimacy with mentioning of God." There is another, deeper state which they call "intimacy with God." In this state one is completely freed from any concern for anything but Him, remaining continuously turned to Him with the sensations of all one's spiritual faculties, and constantly breathing His presence without ever thinking of anything or anyone other than Him. In a blessed, figurative saying which is related as a *hadith qudsi*—the Prophetic saying whose meaning was inspired in the Prophet's heart directly by God—God says: "I am together with one who mentions Me and I am an intimate friend of one who has acquired intimacy with Me." In another narration in which Prophet David, upon him be peace, is addressed, it is said: "O David! Yearn for Me and acquire intimacy with Me. Part company with all else other than Me." We should understand that by the phrase "parting company with" or "keeping apart from all else than God Almighty," the travelers of the path to God should not feel any concern for anything or anyone but God on account of that thing or person itself. Nothing has an existence independent of Him and everything depends on His Names and Attributes. For this reason, those who have true knowledge of God always perceive the Names in whatever there is in the universe and feel a form of relationship with the creation on account of the Names Which are the source of their existence; thus they are gradually freed from other connections and are able to turn to the All-Sacred Being called by the Names, beginning to breathe "intimacy with mention of God" and "intimacy with God."

Imam al-Ghazzali[17] reminds us that intimacy with God is an exalted position which every traveler toward God cannot attain; he tells us the following:

> Every hero who attempts to reach God
> cannot grasp intimacy with God;
> Even those who resort to every means
> they can find cannot perceive it.
> Those of intimacy with God are all noble,
> generous, purified heroes;
> They always work and act purely for the sake of God.[18]

Those who have intimacy with God are the favorites of the realms beyond heavens and the most fortunate among those with nearness to God. They have traversed the distance that originates from their own selves, felt His nearness to everything, enjoyed special compliments as the ones who have reached Him, and have been firmly established in His intimacy.

---

17 Imam Abu Hamid Muhammad al-Ghazzali (1058–1111): A major theologian, jurist, and sage who was considered a reviver (of Islam's purity and vitality) during his time. Known in Europe as Algazel, he was the architect of Islam's later development. He wrote many books, the most famous being *Ihyau 'Ulumi'd-Din* ("Reviving the Religious Sciences"). (Tr.)

18 *Ihyau Ulumi'd-Din* (Turkish trans.), 4:340.

In the state of intimacy that is beyond any measure, Divine manifestations are always felt on different wavelengths. It sometimes happens that certain manifestations of Divine Majesty touch and stroke the faculties of those who have reached Him, during which they feel enveloped with feelings of fear and awe. After a time, there is a period in which the manifestations of His Grace surround them, and at this time they find themselves with more profound sensations of intimacy. In the former state, those who have reached Him tremble and shake like trees and turn pale like the leaves turning in the fall. When faced by the showers of the latter sort of manifestation, they breathe: "I have found the honey of all honey, the source of all honey; let whatever I have be plundered." In an atmosphere in which they continuously feel and experience new instances of attention and favors, they regard everything, including their own selves, as being among that which is other than Him, and thus try to keep distant even from themselves. Even if they live among people, they never get entangled in any veil, and hear, see, and speak about Him alone. They even avoid imagining anything that is transient or bound to decay, their eyes are closed to anything other than His Light, they regard any speeches that are not about Him as empty words, and react against any manners, speeches, or acts that do not remind of Him or cause to be aware of Him or increase the relationship with Him. Whenever they hear a speech or see an action that is not related to Him, they feel as if their heart was bleeding.

Those distinguished with true knowledge of God always preserve their respectful attitude both in the state of meeting with Him and intimacy with Him. They are always in a state of fear, due reverence, and awe. Whatever state they are in, they manifest good manners and modesty. Even though they sometimes feel a tendency toward affectation and utterances that do not comply with the essentials of the Religion in the face of the compassionate and complimentary manifestations of Divine Grace, they immediately tremble and pull themselves together due to their continuous awareness and self-possession, bowing in utter respect and assuming the manners that are required by their positions.

All that we have been trying so far to explain concerning "the one who has attained or reached" are certain features of the states of those who have reached the end of their spiritual journey and met with God. Those who do not experience or taste these cannot perceive or know them, and it is not known to what extent those who know reveal what they know. The sweetness of the honey can only be perceived when the honey is tasted, the smell of a rose is only sensed when the rose is smelt, and the spiritual states can only be known when they are experienced. A friend of the Ultimate Truth expresses his experiences to those who have not had these experiences as follows:

> If you are a weeping nightingale, come to the rose-garden;
> Attain fresh fragrance from the fresh roses.

> O God! I ask you for belief which has penetrated my heart and certainty which does not mislead, so that I may know certainly that nothing but what You have preordained will not happen to me; and bestow blessing and peace on Prophet Muhammad and His family and Companions.

KHUSHU AND *HURMA*
(REVERENT AWE AND RESPECT)

It is a significant attainment and Divine favor that one is able to utterly annihilate themselves in respect of their carnality and egotism and traverses the distance originating in oneself and realizes "meeting with God" and "intimacy with Him." However, it should not be overlooked that like all attainments, this may have certain negative effects on human faculties, for this horizon is the horizon where the dazzling signs of the most transcending and deepest meanings and metaphysical mysteries beyond all sight, hearing, imagination, and conception become completely manifested. Those who have reached this peak can neither discern nor discriminate between the things and events that they have so far seen, heard, and have come to know, nor conclude true judgments concerning them. Therefore, just as it is possible for someone in this state to fall into confusion, so too it is almost inevitable that they make some utterances which are not in compliance with reality. Even though those who seek refuge in the gracious assistance of God Almighty in every step and perceive safety and salvation as being found in dependence on the way of the master of creation, upon him be peace and blessings, are an exception, this risk has always been present. For when the Absolute Sovereign, Who has the absolute right to be "seen," heard, recognized, known and mentioned, makes Himself felt wholly with His nearness, meeting and intimacy, everyone whose capacity and subconscious have not been perfected with the attitudes such as heart-felt veneration and reverent awe finds themselves left powerless to remain as themselves or to express themselves in a rational manner. Since those who have reached such a peak always live in intoxication in parallel with the height of their line of perfection, they frequently act led by these instinctive sensations and cannot discriminate their right hand from their left nor their front from their back.

In such an unusual state, those who are by nature open to intoxication and absorption trespass the limits drawn by the subconscious formed of good manners, respect, and reverent awe, and can go so far as to make utterances such as: "Glory be to me! How supreme my essential character is!" Some others, who only weigh the annihilation of everything in the lights of God's Existence on the scales of the spiritual state and experience cannot help but utter: "I am the Ultimate Truth!" But it is not possible to reconcile this with the respect and manners that all must have before God Almighty. There are still others who breathe the following words, which we can regard as the expression of both the spiritual state and experience and self-possession and respect:

> The space where I am has developed into no-space
> and there has been left no trace of me;
> There is neither anything of my body nor anything of my soul;
> I am from the clime of my Beloved.
> I have discarded both of my eyes so that I see this world
> and the next fused into one single world.
> What I know is one, what I see is one,
> what I speak of is one, what I seek is one.
>
> Mawlana Jalalu'd-Din ar-Rumi[19]

Still others, enchanted by the feeling of attraction, the majesty of perceiving the Divine presence, and the awe of Divine manifestations, speak as follows in the intoxication of the wine of love:

> A call has come to me from the Ultimate Truth:
> "Come, O lover, you are intimate with Us!
> This is the place of intimacy;

---

19 Jalalud-Din ar-Rumi, Mawlana (Mevlana) (1207–1273): One of the most renowned figures of Islamic Sufism. He was the founder of the Mawlawi (Mevlevi) Order of the whirling dervishes, and famous for his *Mathnawi*, an epic of religious life in six volumes. For Western readers, ar-Rumi is a powerful voice among the poets of Sufism. (Tr.)

> I have found you a faithful one!"
> The place where I am has developed into no-space;
> This body of mine has wholly become a soul;
> God's Sight has manifested Itself to me;
> And I have found myself intoxicated with His meeting.[20]

There are still others who refer to "annihilation in God" and "subsistence by and with God" in a relatively more sober style, thus displaying a different state according to the content of their subconscious, saying:

> I have submitted whatever I had to that Friend,
> so I no longer have a house;
> I have been liberated from everything,
> so I have nothing in the name of the two worlds.
> For God's love has reached me and attracted me to itself;
> It has opened the eye of my heart,
> so I am no longer intoxicated.

Ahmedi[21]

The saintly, purified scholars, on the other hand, such as Junayd al-Baghdadi, who traveled in the light of the Prophetic lamp, always acted with self-possession, breathed with reverent awe, and their eyes twinkled with heart-felt veneration, without causing those who were incapable of traveling a spiritual path to fall into confusion or deviation. Some other close friends of God, such as ash-Shibli[22] and those of a similar disposition, revealed their sensations under the influence of their nature, and caused those who had no connection with spiri-

---

20 Imadu'd-Din Nasimi (1369–1417), Azerbaijan's outstanding poet of the 15th century, wrote in Turkish along with Arabic and Persian. He was very successful in lyric poems. (Tr.)

21 Emir Muhammed ibn Emir Ahmedi lived in the same age as Jalalu'd-Din ar-Rumi. He lived in Bayburt, in the Eastern Turkey. He was also the leader of the *Ahi*s (The Brotherhood of Craftsmen and Tradesmen) in the region. (Tr.)

22 Abu Bakr ash-Shibli, of Khorasan by origin but born in Baghdad or Samarra, son of a court official and himself promoted in the imperial service, as Governor of Demavend. However, giving up governorship, he joined the circle of Junayd al-Baghdadi, and became one of the leading figures in Islamic Sufism. He died in 846 at the age of 87. (Tr.)

tuality to be informed of certain secrets, thus providing an opportunity to criticize both these people and their way. However, they never behaved improperly or displayed disrespect in adherence to the essentials of the journey. As for the people of heart, such as al-Hallaj,[23] as-Suhrawardi[24] and Ibnu'l-Farid,[25] although they were sincere in their love and yearning, and were favored with a certain degree of attraction and the feeling of being attracted, they were not able to act with self-possession, due to their continuous intoxication and absorption, nor to remain distant from improper utterances that would cause misunderstanding, thus laying some ground for certain reckless acts and manners.

The true heirs to the Prophetic way have always traveled in self-possession, weighing up their visions and inner sensations on the balance of the Sunna, evaluating their spiritual unveilings according to the established truths and criteria of the Religion, and doing their utmost in order not to lead the common people into confusion. While they have attached great importance to nearness to God, they also have tried to show utmost respect in their relationship with Him, and have preserved their good manners, heartfelt veneration and reverent awe. Over time, with the reflection of their heart-felt veneration and reverence in their everyday acts, behavior, and words, they have become heroes of self-possession and the representation of Islam, acting as examples for others in their relations with both the Creator and the created.

---

23 Husayn ibn Mansur al-Hallaj (244/857–309/922) was one of the most famous of Muslim Sufis. He was born in Shushtar in western Iran and lived in Baghdad. He is famous for his utterance "I am the Truth." He is also famous for his austerities.

24 Shihabu'd-Din Abu Hafs 'Umar ibn 'Abdullah as-Suhrawardi (1145–1234) was a Sufi theologian. *'Awarif al-Ma'arif* is about the Sufi way. He also criticized the philosophers following the ancient Greek Philosophy. (Tr.)

25 'Umar ibnu'l-Farid (1181–1235) is one of the most venerated poets in Arabic, whose expression of Sufi experiences is regarded as the finest in the Arabic language. He studied for a legal career but abandoned law for a solitary religious life in the Muqattam hills near Cairo. He spent some years in or near Makka, where he met the renowned Sufi as-Suhrawardi. (Tr.)

Their hearts, where their perception of God's Grandeur, Majesty, and Dominion were combined with their admission of their innate impotence, poverty, neediness and essential nothingness, always beat with utmost respect and adoration. This state was manifest in their acts and speeches. They always acted properly and preserved their good manners and respect both at the beginning and at the end of the path, breathing reverent awe and remaining humble and modest even when they reached the level of angels. However, this does not mean that all of them were of the same level in their knowledge of God. Rather, there were considerable differences among them in this respect. Among them were those who pulled themselves together and bent double in reverent awe whenever they remembered God, and there were those who breathed self-possession and vigilance with the consideration that God saw them in whatever state they were or with whatever task they busied themselves, as they spent their life in complete awareness of God's omnipresence.

In whatever stage of the journey and at whatever degree of certainty they may be, a traveler toward God should never fall short of reverent awe and heart-felt veneration. It should be pointed out here that having reverent awe is different from appearing to have it. God always wants His servants to try their hardest to deny themselves in profound modesty and the admission of their essential impotence and poverty, thus confirming Him with His absolute Power and Riches. Appearing to have more reverence and awe than one really feels in their heart is hypocrisy and disrespect for God. If reverent awe is a requirement of servanthood to God—and there is no doubt that it is—it is the arm or wing of the traveler in their journey toward the Ultimate Truth; it is their greenhouse and their shield, their safety belt and lifeline. Those who advance with such an arm or wing, who manage to enter this greenhouse and use this shield well as a means of Divine protection, those who fasten this safety belt and hold fast to this lifeline continuously advance on the path without slipping; they are able to act in self-possession and show respect to God on the path that goes towards Him. When they reach the end of the path by which they can meet and achieve intimacy with Him, they are under the influence of this subconscious attainment, which they have developed into a significant depth of their nature. For they have come to know what they should know—they have come to know this in the way the heroes of knowledge of God know. As declared in the verse, *Of all His servants, only those possessed of true knowledge stand in awe of God* (35:28), only those who are able to recognize or know Him with His Attributes of Glory and All-Beautiful Names and who are able to travel in the horizon of living as if seeing God or in awareness of the fact that God sees whatever we do and say, are able to feel the required respect, reverence, and adoration for God in whatever state they may be. However, they differ in the degree of their knowledge according to the capacity and certainty of each.

A servant's self-possession and adoration of God and their manners are proportionate to their recognition and knowledge of God. The most knowledgeable of the knowledgeable, upon him be peace and blessings, reminds of this fact by saying: "I am the one who has the greatest awe of God and who is the most God-conscious."[26] The conclusion of the verse mentioned above also corroborates this. The conclusive statement, *Surely God is All-Glorious with irresistible might, All-Forgiving*, which combines hope and fear and encouragement (toward good) and discouragement (from evil), moves the spirit with feelings of reverent awe, respect, and adoration. For the *All-Forgiving* gives the glad tidings of pardon and brings relief, while the *All-Glorious with irresistible might* warns that God has the power to do whatever He wills, is absolutely undefeatable and irresistible, and is the sole Sovereign on the throne of sovereignty. Therefore, in accordance with the Qur'anic declaration, *(He) feels awe of the All-Merciful, though unseen (beyond their perception)* (36:11), a traveler toward God's presence who is to be honored with vision of Him always considers His Majesty and Grandeur, trembles and never abandons themselves to carelessness with the excuse that God is the All-Merciful. At the same instant, when such a traveler

---

26 *(Sahihu'l)-Bukhari*, "Nikah" 1; Ibn Hibban, *as-Sahih*, 2:20.

thinks of God's being the All-Forgiving and the All-Compassionate, they are startled by the pronouncement, *I surely am the All-Forgiving, the All-Compassionate, and My punishment—it is indeed the painful punishment* (15:49–50), and they always breathe with feelings of reverent awe and heart-felt veneration.

In addition to being a safety belt for those who are at the beginning of the path, reverent awe and heart-felt veneration are a powerful dynamo of warning for the heroes of intimacy with God in the horizon of meeting with Him, acting as a break against recklessness and improper utterances. It is only with this feeling that while those who are at the beginning of the path can traverse the most dangerous stages of the journey with the least difficulty and without being entangled in anything, those who have reached the end of the path can fulfill what is due to their position and are saved from the pitfall of changing meeting into separation and intimacy into isolation.

Whoever one is, to the extent that one is able to make their spirit feel heart-felt veneration and reverent awe, they are neither shaken by tedious fear of others nor do they have to bow before them in worry. As a matter of fact, in addition to ordering us to love Him and love others only on account of Him, God Almighty wants us to channel our feelings of fear into fear and reverent awe of Him. The Divine command, *Do not fear them but fear Me!* (3:175) is sufficiently explicit in this respect.

The following lines by the author of *Lujja* beautifully express the same point:

> If you fear the punishment of God,
> establish yourself in the Religion more firmly;
> Trees are rooted more firmly in the ground
> for fear of violent storms.

There are ignorant ones who are unaware of where the path they are following in the world is leading them. They eat, drink, sleep and finally roll down into the pit of death which has been formed by their life and opinions of life and death.

There are others who see knowledge, religious acts and responsibilities and the end that awaits them in a murky, smoky, misty way, as if they are observing them from behind a foggy piece of glass. They have neither knowledge of the beginning and end of the world nor fear or reverent awe. When it is time to die after a life spent in indecision, they are dragged to their pitiable end with their shaky belief and actions.

There are still others who advance toward their end with knowledge and actions and act dependent on certain degrees of knowledge of God. They sometimes breathe with love, but since they are unaware of heart-felt veneration and reverent awe and are unable to adorn their actions with sincerity, they confuse white and black with one another and usually leave the world suffering losses, despite the opportunities to gain they were given.

There are still others: they have perfect knowledge, knowledge of God, and love, and travel their path in sincerity. However, since they suffer from a lack of sufficient fear and reverent awe, they may feel dizzied by some attainments. Even though they maintain their position by acting in accordance with it, they may display carefree attitudes and make improper utterances that cannot be reconciled with modesty, humility, and the sense of nothingness that are the foundations of servanthood to God. They provide material for certain frivolous souls.

For this reason, all believers, in particular those who have dedicated themselves to the Ultimate Truth, should scrutinize themselves in respect of fear and awe at every step of their journey, examining to what extent reverent awe and heart-felt veneration have become a part of their subconscious so that they may be preserved from carefree acts and manners and not darken the way of gain with loss. The author of *Mizanu'l-'Irfan*[27] says the following things in this respect:

---

[27] The author of *Mizanu'l-'Irfan* is Mustafa Fevzi ibn Nu'man (d. 1924). The author was a writer and poet following the Naqshbandi way. He was among the disciples of Hasan Hilmi (1825–1912), a famous 19th century Turkish Sufi guides. (Tr.)

O initiate, make your soul know fear,
so that your soul may weep with fear.
The debased soul should fear God so much so that
it should be left weak and helpless.
The low-down soul should not be carefree,
thus impelling you to act freely.
Believers do not speak recklessly,
nor do they dare not fulfill their duty.
Be always fearful of the Ultimate Truth,
and let your knowledge of Him lead you.

Heart-felt veneration, reverent awe, and the feelings of fear and awe which they generate in the heart are extraordinarily important for everyone, and are not only the most significant fruit of true belief, but are also the most valuable result of certainty that is bestowed on a person due to their continuous turning to God. A hero of truth who has been able to pick up this fruit and obtain this result can be regarded as having gained everything they can be expected to. For since they have turned faithfully to the Being Who has the reins of everything in His Hand, they are a candidate to be favored with all His gifts. In a saying that is related as a *hadith qudsi*, our Prophet, upon him be peace and blessings, declares:

> God Almighty says to His servant: "Make a present of your heart-felt reverence and the tears of your eyes to Me, and then ask Me for the gratification of whatever needs you have so that I may answer your call. For I am near and I answer the call of everyone who prays to Me."

> O God! We ask You for whatever good Your Prophet Muhammad, upon him be peace and blessings, asked You for, and we seek refuge in You from whatever evil Your Prophet Muhammad, upon him be peace and blessings, sought refuge in You from. We ask you for everything good, whether immediate or postponed, and we seek refuge in You from everything evil, whether immediate or postponed. We ask You for Paradise and whatever word and action which will make us near to it, and we seek refuge in You from Hell and whatever word and action which will make us near to it. Amen! And bestow blessings and peace on our master Muhammad and on his Family and Companions, altogether.

THE HORIZON OF "THE SECRET"
AND WHAT LIES BEYOND

I am aware that I am not able to write and speak about this topic as it should be written and spoken about. My pen and words also tell me this. I suffer from keeping silent and not writing anything, while writing or speaking about a matter that is beyond my capacity of perception and expression is a venture that I take on with trepidation. However, I have been able neither to keep silent nor be relieved of the anxieties that my writings have generated in my spirit. Having always regarded my inability and neediness as a call for God's help, and my venture as a signal to incite people of endeavor and devotion whose hearts dominate their tongues, whose tongues translate their "secret," whose "secret" is open to their horizon of "private," and whose "private" is connected to their "more private," I have uttered "In and with the Name of God," and "from God," and "toward God," and I advance asking for God's extra grace.

For those who can understand, I have always admitted that I am not a person who is able to write or speak about this profound topic and similar, other simpler ones. But I am convinced that these topics, which have so far formed three published volumes and will possibly form a new fourth one, should be discussed. During all my daring attempts to write about them, I have wept with my pen, sometimes with yearning, and sometimes shuddering. While my pen has breathed with the ink it pours forth, I have breathed with my tears. It is the Creator Who knows my heart and has perfect knowledge of my "secret;" it is again He Who knows the truths of "the private" and "the more private," and Who makes them known by whomever He wills, and it is He Who graciously protects and helps those who narrate what they read and hear.

Literally meaning something kept hidden, *sir* ("the secret"), which was discussed before,[28] is a heavenly faculty belonging to the heart. The secret has the same meaning for the heart as the spirit for the body. Meaning something concealed and imperceptible, *khafi* ("the private") is another deep dimension of the heart which is turned to the realms and truths beyond those to which "the secret" is turned, and another observatory from which we can look on the truths. As for *akhfa* ("the more private"), which literally means something more hidden, more obscure, and more profound for perceiving, it is a window which is open to further and further realms and truths and through which God's gifts pour.

According to some friends of the Ultimate Truth, "the spirit" is an element through which one loves and has a relationship with God Almighty; "the heart" is a storehouse of the knowledge of God; "the secret" is a system with which we can observe more abstract and profound truths by His grace, while "the private" is a design or map of Divine mysteries, and "the more private" is a mysterious key with which to open the Hidden Treasure. Without God's grace and assistance, it would not be possible to know the true nature of these faculties. Although with his secret, private, and more private every believer has the potential to have certain knowledge of the Attributes and Essence of God, as well as the Divine mysteries and the Hidden Treasure, it is not possible for human free will to set these faculties in action without Divine leave or help. Human beings are able to see by God's causing us to see, to hear by His causing us to hear, and to feel by His causing us to feel, and are not able to do any of these actions by themselves; in the same way it is impossible for a human being to say anything concerning the Attributes, Essential Qualities or Characteristics, and Essence of

---

[28] It was discussed in the 2nd volume of *Emerald Hills of the Heart*, pp. 66–70. (Tr.)

the Divine Being without God's help or grace. God Almighty has perfect knowledge of every human being, including their spirit, heart, secret, private and more private. He has perfect knowledge of everything, be it of particular or universal character. He enables whomever He will to know whatever part of His knowledge He wills to be known, while He keeps unknown whatever part He wills to remain unknown. Concerning His Knowledge the Qur'an tells us: *He knows whatever is in their hearts* (48:18); *Surely I know all that you do not know* (2:30); *I know well all that you reveal and all that you have been keeping secret* (2:33); *Know that surely God knows whatever is in your souls* (2:235) *Do they (the hypocrites) not know that God knows what they keep concealed and their private counsels and gossips, and that God has full knowledge of the whole of the Unseen?* (9:78). Without His making known, human beings would not even be able to know themselves, let alone know what lies behind the secret.

Since the creation of humanity, it is only with God's special guidance and assistance that humanity has been able to read whatever is to be read correctly concerning the outer and inner world. Whenever humanity has remained indifferent to His guidance and illumination, it has continuously faltered and been dragged into hesitation, and it has not been able to say a true word, particularly about the Divine Essence, Attributes, and Names. Whenever people have opened their mouths to utter something, they have only been able to utter nonsense.

God Almighty has kept us informed about His Essence, Attributes, and Names by means of His distinguished servants, known as "the perfectly purified, chosen ones, the truly good" (38:47). We have tried to perceive these transcending matters in keeping with their instructions and thereby have been saved from falling into hesitation or conflict. During times when we have remained deaf to the instructions and enlightenments of the true guides, such as the Prophets, saints, and the purified, saintly scholars, we have been neither able to grasp the truth nor preserve the balance concerning the matters of transcending character. It is the Divine Being Who knows Himself, while others can have knowledge of Him only to the extent He makes known. Confirming this point, our master, upon him be peace and blessings, declares: "I know my Lord by my Lord." This Prophetic saying is of great significance, particularly in respect of teaching us that the Divine Being is beyond our scope of perception or knowledge, and it is the Divine Being alone Who is the unique source of all true knowledge.

Returning to our main discussion, the secret is, as mentioned before, the initial point of observing and studying the truth and what lies beyond it. According to their capacity and the horizon of their knowledge of Divinity, every believer can read, evaluate, and interpret the mysteries concerning the Creator and the created through this depth of their heart by God's leave and help and with the signs, markers, and signposts that He has laid out.

The private is a horizon of observing the realms of existence and non-existence together from above; it is a receiver for those who are elect for special regard and favors, and a particular depth of the heart that will enable them to look through on the mysteries of Divinity and the things or beings that have not yet been brought into or have been sent from the physical existence. It is an exceptional gift of the Unique, Eternally Besought One to humans.

As for the more private, as an incomparable gift from God's grace it is the most important dimension of a heart which is open to the Hidden Treasure, a heavenly faculty.

Those favored with the secret and those distinguished with the private and those honored and exalted with the more private receive the gifts flowing down onto their horizons, the presents offered to their highest point of perfection, and the showers of inspiration that descend to their atmosphere; they consider them and reveal whatever of these and to whatever extent they are allowed to reveal to those who are qualified to receive them; the rest they keep concealed, without giving any secrets to those who cannot understand or keep them. This is what the Prophets and the purified, saintly scholars of verification have done. They are the captivating translators of the Divine will; they depend on the eternal Criterion in all their words and actions. As for those who confuse the rulings and commandments of the Name the All-Outward with the mysteries of the Name the All-Inward, even though they are among the heroes of nearness to God, since they depend on their own vision and unveilings in interpreting the truths, and are content with their own sensations and experiences, and since they are therefore not able to weigh up the results of their visions or observations in the balance of the Sunna, they not only fall but also cause others to fall into confusion; they cause others to make faults by revealing certain Divine mysteries which they are not allowed to reveal due to oblivion and intoxication, eventually losing their life or becoming the targets of severe reprimands or being condemned in the public view.

It is true that God Almighty has sometimes revealed certain mysteries of His Essence, Attributes and Names. But He has done so within the framework of certain causes as a requirement of His Dignity and Grandeur, and He has offered them from behind certain veils. For this reason, what befalls the loyal servants at the door of the Ultimate Truth is not to manifest whatever vision or unveiling with which they have been favored, thus avoiding throwing the masses into confusions and wrong actions. There is safety in silence and respect for the Ultimate Truth in not revealing Divine mysteries. A time comes for one who has reached the end of the path when all Divine Attributes and Names are eclipsed by the lights of the Divine Essence. This is the horizon of *All things are perishable except His Face* (28:88). Like everything else, the corporeal existence of the servant, which is entrusted to the servant, is also eclipsed and becomes invisible. This transient, death-bound design is completely surrounded by the lights of the All-Permanent Existence and only the signals of the manifestation of the Divine Essence are experienced. This spiritual experience has been described as the Ultimate Truth making the hidden manifest.

The favors that emerge on the horizon of the private depend on one's freedom from selfhood. For this reason, those who are at the beginning of the spiritual journey are not able to be familiar with the manifestations of the True Existence unless they are freed from their "figurative" existence. Those who see themselves as their own owners can neither reach the horizon of "the private" nor rise to the peak where the mysteries of Divine Lordship can be observed nor receive the fragrance of the Hidden Treasure. The mysteries of the Hidden Treasure are revealed on the horizon of "the more private." This mysterious realm that is beyond the realm of mysteries is a horizon which is particular primarily to the one who is the nearest of all to the Divine Being, upon him be peace and blessings, and then to the other servants at His door in accordance with their adherence to the Prophetic way. Those who have not experienced the secret or drunk sips from the cup of the private can never rise to this peak. Just as those who have stuck fast to the wording can never discover the meaning, neither can those who only concentrate on the meaning ever attain familiarity with the essence or arrive at the truth. Supposing the impossible, even if they do arrive at the truth somehow, they can never get a glimpse of the Truth of the truths.

The Truth of the truths is the unique source and foundation of everything. Those who feel and experience It have grasped everything, while those who cannot find It continuously suffer tiredness and spend their life in vain. The Hidden Treasure is another title of the treasure of the mystery of Oneness and the absolutely Unseen, which cannot be grasped not only by ordinary people but also by those who have reached the horizons of the heart and the secret, and even for those who are the more advanced in experiencing the private. Everything in the name of existence and favor originates in this all-transcending horizon and descends downward, developing branches until it reaches us. It is the original beginning, because everything ends in It, while humankind, which is the fruit of creation, is the result. This may also be called "the manifestation in the form of descent." Our horizon as corporeal beings is the start of the journey realized toward the Hidden Treasure through further and further realms; this is achieved by setting the systems of the heart and spirit into action, while the more private is the end or end point. This journeying is the ascent or ascension.

God's saintly friends usually say: "The womb is related to or has connection with the realm of Knowledge." This may be interpreted to mean that everything has an original existence in Divine Knowledge, and that these known entities or elements of Knowledge proceed toward external existence through certain, pre-ordained stages of identification or specification in order to function as mirrors of the All-Pure Existence. In other words, everything has a hidden existence that is free of time and space in the Hidden Treasure. In the initial stage of existence, they are individually identified in Knowledge, and then they are honored with spiritual existence. Finally, they are favored with the garment of subtle and corporeal existence. These are roughly the three stages of coming into corporeal existence. This process is described as a favor of descent, while the spiritual journeying upward through the heart and the spirit, or the heart and the secret, or the secret and the private, or the private and the more private is called ascent or ascension.

The horizon of the more private is an exceptional rank or realm that is particular to the way of Prophet Muhammad, upon him be peace and blessings. Those who do not follow this way cannot reach this peak. The final point that they can attain is the secret or the private. This is the end point of their rise that their capacity allows them to reach. Each of the steps at these peaks is also the point where the genuine nature of a Prophet is projected and marks the line of his spiritual journeying. Those who journey along the same line or are favored with the observation of truths from the same horizon seem to be the representatives of some basic qualities particular to that Prophet. It is because of this subtle reality that there may appear among those representatives ones who confuse the original with the representation and therefore claim to have a part in the Prophethood of that Prophet; or some of the followers of those representatives may attribute to their masters partnership in the Prophethood in question. However, how can the light of the moon or the reflection of the sun in bubbles can be compared with the sun itself?

According to the Sufis, the original owners of the highest ranks in question are the greatest of the Prophets, such as Prophet Adam, Prophet Abraham, Prophet Moses, and Prophet Jesus, upon them be peace. According to the Sufis, the sole, unique master of the horizon of the more private is the Seal of the Mission of Prophethood, upon him be perfect blessings and peace. The rise of the Prophets from the beginning to the end was through a sudden, instantaneous Divine attraction. Others have to follow their way, even when they are favored with Divine attraction. Believers advance on the spiritual path in adherence to its disciplines, sipping at knowledge of God with a new observation with every step from the spirit to the heart, and from the heart to the secret, and from the secret to the private, and from the private to the more private. They are cooled by being washed in the most profound and enjoyable of spiritual pleasures; they experience new types of intoxication through the mysteries of Divine Acts; they observe different manifestations in the horizon of Divine Names; they encounter surprise after surprise in the atmosphere of Divine Attributes of Glory; they undergo changes and transformations through the mysteries of Divinity; they ultimately reach the final point in their rise according to their capacity.

The perfections acquired along the path through the realm of the initial manifestations of Divine Commands are preliminary to the gifts and ranks that are to be obtained in the realm of creation. The former journey (which is in the realm of the initial manifestation of Divine Commands) is the path of sainthood, while the latter (which is realized in the realm of creation) is the ascension of Prophethood. This also shows that sainthood serves Prophethood and it was a step toward it in Prophets. A saint advances and rises in order to find a new thing at every step, and thus deepens in what they have found, while a Prophet stands at the intersection of the realms of the initial manifestation of Divine Commands and creation in order to lead others to find what he has found according to the individual capacity. He lays paths from multiplicity to unity and weaves a lace of spirituality from matter. Although his mission encompasses all the peculiarities of the realm of the initial manifestation of Divine Commands, it fundamentally relates to the realm of creation. With the exception of the pillars of belief, which originally belong to the realm of the initial manifestation of Divine Commands, all the orders and prohibitions of Islam, the bounties of Paradise, the punishment of Hell, the happiness of the vision of God in Paradise, and the delight of relationships being established with those near to God constitute the essence of the basic messages of the Prophets and relate to the realm of creation.

All the acts incumbent on the Muslims in the age of responsibility, and all the principles of being advantageous or disadvantageous also relate to the realm of creation and are the fruits and greenhouses provided by the horizon of Prophethood. The regular, optional recitations, and the actions of the heart, such as self-criticism, self-supervision, and reflection, which are regarded as provisions on the way of sainthood, support the basic commandments of the Religion and the essential duties of the religious life. The negligence and failure in the latter is the cause of the deprivation of the blessings of the former, while those who fulfill the latter completely do not make lasting faults in the performance of the former. The nearness to God which the way of Prophethood enables through the fulfillment of obligations is essential, while the nearness obtained on the way of sainthood through supererogatory acts is of a secondary nature. If something essential is fulfilled accurately, that which is of secondary nature is subordinated to it.

> O God! Revive us through obligatory acts and duties and make us alive in them. Adorn us with supererogatory acts and duties and make us near to You. Bestow blessings and peace on our master Muhammad and on his Family and Companions, altogether.

HAQQ (THE TRUTH), HAQIQA (THE GENUINE) AND WHAT LIES BEYOND

Literally meaning what is true, established, or constant, *haqq* (the truth) denotes that an utterance, an act, or a creed is totally in agreement with what is originally true, real, and genuine. Its opposite is *batil* (falsehood). In addition, *haqq* also means that which is immediately perceived when it is seen or heard. When it is mentioned without reference to anything particular, as mentioned in the verse, ... *they will come to know that God it is Who is "al-Haqqu'l-Mubin"* (the All-Clear, Ultimate Truth and Ever-Constant) (24:25), what is being referred to is the Divine Being. God's saintly friends have always meant the Divine Being when they speak of the (Ultimate) Truth.

As for *haqiqa*, which is derived from the same root word as *haqq*, it means the essence and original or exact form of something; that which is genuine and real, not figurative. In Sufi terminology, this is one of the four steps or degrees in the spiritual journey; these consist of the Shari'a (the Divine way or the set of Divine laws), the *tariqa* (the spiritual path or the order which follows a spiritual path), the *haqiqa* (the essence, the genuine), and the *ma'rifa* (knowledge of God).

The Shari'a is all the religious principles which everyone knows or has to know and practice; *tariqa* is the way of experiencing the spiritual depths of the Shari'a through certain particular systems, while *haqiqa* is the attainment of certain mysteries of Divine Names and secrets of Divine Attributes of Glory through certain efforts and practices. Finally, *ma'rifa* is the capacity of and provision for the gift that comes in return for seeking, feeling, and obtaining knowledge of certain subtle, profound truths concerning the Essential Qualities or Characteristics of the Divine Being and the mysteries of Divinity.

According to another approach, *ma'rifa* is a summary of knowledge and a special gift in return for belief in God, while *tariqa* is a way or method to make this attainment, and the Shari'a and *haqiqa* are the names of the goal to be attained. Although the sole goal for a servant is obtaining God's approval and good pleasure, the way to this goal extends through the Shari'a and *haqiqa*, which are two profound dimensions of a single truth.

Shari'a is faithfulness to the mystery of servanthood and living a life in obedience to Divine commands; *haqiqa* is resignation to whatever God decrees and judges as the Lord of the whole creation, and the continuous experience of the principle: "We are pleased with God as the Lord, Islam as religion, and Muhammad as the Messenger." The practice of Shari'a or the order established by Shari'a, if it is not connected to the horizon of *haqiqa*, is barren, while *haqiqa* which is not dependent on or does not originate in Shari'a is futile.

From another perspective, the Shari'a is the set of the responsibilities with which God has charged His servants, and the *haqiqa* is discerning and reading mysteries of Divinity in the Shari'a. As also stated by Abu 'Ali ad-Daqqaq,[29] *You alone do we worship* (1:5) marks observation of the limits of the Shari'a, and *From You alone do we seek help* (1:5) indicates the horizon of *haqiqa*. In short:

> Shari'a and *haqiqa* are one within the other;
> While the *tariqa* is the path leading to this horizon.
> *Ma'rifa* is provision for the travelers on the path,
> Beyond which come faithfulness, sincerity, and endeavor.
>
> Livai

---

29 Abu 'Ali ad-Daqqaq (d. 405AH/1014CE) was one of the leading Sufi masters in the history of Islam. He was taught by Abu 'Abdu'r-Rahman as-Sulami and taught the famous Sufi master, ascetic, and writer Abu'l-Qasim 'Abdu'l-Karim al-Qushayri. (Tr.)

Another approach is that the Shari'a is perfect belief and righteous deeds, while *haqiqa* is God's protection of these heroes of belief and righteous actions, as well as being the response of these heroes to this protection with a universal consciousness. It is a delusion if we expect Divine help and protection without belief and righteous actions; it is extremely difficult to be able to bear the heavy responsibilities of the sacred, noble Shari'a without confidence in God's special regard and help. Some have summed up this reality by saying: "Establishing the Shari'a without *haqiqa* is extremely difficult, while the attainment of *haqiqa* without the Shari'a is impossible."

Within their broader meanings, the Shari'a is the fulfillment of all individual, family, and social responsibilities, while *haqiqa* is acting as if seeing or in awareness of our being always seen by the One Who creates everything and favors each of His creatures with a rank of existence, the One Who creates guidance and misguidance and Who has the authority to guide or mislead whom He wills. It is He Who exalts and honors whom He wills and abases whom He wills, Who bestows success on whom He wills and causes whom He wills to lose, Who exalts whom He wills with dominion and takes away dominion from whom He wills, Who destines and decrees good and evil, belief and unbelief, benefit and harm, success and loss, and Who is referred to in the statement: "Whatever He wills to be is and whatever He wills not to be is not."[30]

From another point of view, the Shari'a is the essentials that are taught and conveyed by noble Prophets for observation, while *haqiqa* is the favor of experiencing these teachings and responsibilities in the heart and spirit or through vision and spiritual observation. Starting from this point of view, some verifying scholars have regarded the observance of the religious commands and prohibitions as the dimension of Shari'a that consists of servanthood to and worship of God, and seen the dimension of *haqiqa*

---

[30] *Abu Dawud*, "Sunna" 6; al-Bayhaqi, *al-I'tiqad*, 1:161.

as the gifts of witnessing, experiencing, and unveiling the profound truths that underlie those commands and prohibitions.

Haqaiq (truths) is the plural of *haqiqa*, and this is dealt with in four degrees. The truths of the first or greatest degree are those concerning the All-Holy Divine Essence. The travelers toward the Ultimate Truth who seek these truths should always be faithful in their thoughts, speeches, and acts to the criteria established by the Legislator of Shari'a, remaining distant from personal comments and interpretations, even though when they are flying at the highest peaks of knowledge of God and spiritual experience. The truths of the second degree are those pertaining to the Divine Attributes of Glory. The travelers advancing toward this horizon should remain within the limits of the knowledge of the Divine Being provided by the All-Beautiful Names and within the framework established by the sacred Attributes. They should refer the knowledge about what lies beyond these limits to His special attention and favors without any personal expectations. The truths of the third degree are those regarding Divine Acts. Those who seek these truths should, provided they attribute to God Almighty everything that exists and occurs in this realm of contingency where Divine Names and Attributes manifest themselves and operate, advance as far as they can in reflection and contemplation of the outer and inner worlds and try to study things and events in the minutest detail several times every day.

The truths of the fourth degree are those pertaining to the works or outcomes of Divine Acts. The realm where all qualities and quantities are manifested, substances and corporeal bodies are formed and dissolve, and all acts of joining, separation, formation, deformation, dissolution, and disappearance occur is the realm of these truths. If a mental travel can be led by sound vision, insight, and discernment in this realm, it becomes possible to attain knowledge and knowledge of God. But if those who travel in this realm in pursuit of the truths in question do not view acts, events, and occurrences through insight and discernment, and if they cannot transcend the sphere of apparent causes, they will inevitably fall into naturalism. In fact, this realm is described as follows:

> The sheets of the book of the universe are of infinite kinds,
> Its individual letters and words are also countless.
> Written in the printing house of the Preserved Tablet of Truth,
> Each creature in the universe is a meaningful embodied word.
>
> Hoja Tahsin[31]

However, those who have not been able to find the true point of view cannot be saved from mistakenly seeing, reading or interpreting it.

Haqiqatu'l-haqaiq (The Truth of truths) is a term which is used to express the rank of Divine absolute Oneness (according to some, the rank of Divine absolute Unity), which is the rank of God's original manifestation in His Essence. Some call this The All-Holy Absorption or the All-Holy Existence, or the Unseen of All Unseen. However, it is not permissible to see this most sublime truth as self-identified or in terms of being or coming into existence as the Pure Essence. Neither can it be regarded or imagined as a relative truth. Just as the Divine Essence cannot also be thought to manifest Himself without a veil, so also the Truth of truths cannot be talked about as purely He without considering His Attributes or Names as veils. We can find way to gain knowledge of Him through His Attributes and Names. The All-Holy Essence of the Divine Being is absolutely free from any descriptions. Any description of Him means putting a limit on Him. It is we who are limited; therefore, it is a religious essential to see the Ultimate Truth in His Own position and the created in its own position. Any other approach would be clear misguidance and bewilderment. The duty which falls on servants is turning to God in utter submission and trying to

---

31 Hoja Hasan Tahsin (1811–1881) was one of the leading thinkers and educationalists of the 19th century Ottoman Turkey. He was the first director of *Daru'l-Funun* (Istanbul University). He was well-versed religious sciences and had great learning of natural sciences. (Tr.)

traverse their distance from Him, advancing toward that All-In-comprehensible One in the guidance of the sacred, noble Shari'a and with the provision of knowledge of Him. Concerning this top-ic, a friend of God says as follows:

> Flee, O initiate, from the realm of multiplicity; advance!
> Settling firmly in the Court of the All-Independent,
> Unique One, advance!
> If you desire to see the Face of Oneness through this multiplicity,
> Purify and brighten the mirror of your heart; advance!
> Some continuously turn around the Ka'ba,
> some around the Divine Throne;
> You prefer the sacred sanctuary of God's nearness; advance!
> There is no end to the journey of those who set out toward Him;
> Wherever you reach, go beyond; advance!
>
> Ismail Haqqi[32]

In reality, there is no end to the journey toward the All-Infinite One. Visions and experiences which take a whole life-time will con-tinue in different depths both in this world and the next. An initi-ate who has been dedicated to such a journey will run from one vi-sion or observation to another, perceiving from different perspec-tives, even though they have been honored with His meeting and company; possibly they will be transported by the pleasure of vi-sion and observation many times a day.

> O God! I ask You for resignation after calamity or any of Your decrees or judgments concerning me, the coolness of life after death, the pleasure of observing Your Face, and the zeal to meet You without suffering the harm of anything harmful, or any mis-leading intrigue and mischief. And bestow, O Lord, blessings and peace on the Inaugurator and Seal of Prophethood, on his Family and Companions, may God be pleased with them all.

---

32 Ismail Haqqi Bursavi (1653–1725) is one of the great Sufi guides and writers. He spent much of his life in Bursa, Turkey. His *Ruhu'l-Bayan* (a 4-volume commentary on the Qur'an) is very famous. *Kitabu'n-Natica* ("The Book on the Result") is his last work. (Tr.)

GOD AND THE TRUTH OF DIVINITY

The sacred term *Allah* (God), which is also referred to as the Word of Majesty or the All-Supreme Name in the sense that it is the Chief Divine Name comprising all other Names, is the proper Name of the All-Majestic, All-High Divine Being, Who introduces Himself to us with His All-Beautiful Names and draws a frame in our minds with all His Attributes of Glory so that we may have knowledge of Him; He is the All-Sacred One called by all His Names and the All-Glorified One described by all His Attributes of Perfection, and it is He Who is the sole, peerless Sovereign on the Thrones of Divinity and Lordship. As also stated by Sayyid Sharif al-Jurjani,[33] the all-blessed word of God is the proper Name of the Divine Essence as God, (from the viewpoint of His absolute Uniqueness and His total detachment from the created). According to the scholars of the basic principles of the Religion and the religious methodology, *Allah* (God) is a proper Name particular to the Divine Essence exclusively. Known also as the Name of Majesty and the All-Supreme or Greatest Name, this all-blessed Word is particularly mentioned as the Greatest or All-Supreme Name.

All the other Names belonging to the Divine Being are descriptive names or the names or titles that function like attributes, while the word *Allah* (God) is the Name of His Essence (*Dhat*), and comprises all the other Names directly or indirectly. That is to say, if a person declares their belief with the expressions such as "There is no deity but the All-Holy and All-Pure," or "There is no deity but

---

33 Sayyid Sharif al-Jurjani (d. 1413): One of the leading theologians of the 15th century. He visited Istanbul in 1374, and upon his return, in 1377, he was given a teaching appointment in Shiraz. *Sharhu'l-Mawaqif* is his most famous work. (Tr.)

the All-Compassionate," or "There is no deity but the All-Glorious with irresistible might," and so on, they have not declared their belief properly, as none of these Names wholly designate the Divine Being, Who is known by all His Names and recognized by all His Attributes. One who declares their belief only with such expressions knowingly or unknowingly attempts to restrict the infinite sphere of Divinity and Lordship to the areas of the manifestations of the Names the All-Holy and All-Pure or the All-Compassionate or the All-Glorious with irresistible might, thus trying to make the infinite finite or the all-encompassing encompassed in one respect.

The All-Majestic, All-High Being Who is called by the all-sacred Name God[34] is the unique source of the truths of humanity, the universe, and things, and their ultimate, unique origin and ultimate, unique, primary cause. He is the Necessarily Existent Being Who exists by Himself. All our studies of the outer and our inner worlds demonstrate this fact. There is not a single thing in the universe that does not have multiple indications of the All-Sacred One Who is called by the Name of Glory, God. It can be said that the All-Sacred Name God exists inscribed both on the face of every thing and being and on the visage of the universe as a whole. However, this truth is more manifest and more clearly eligible in the physical and metaphysical face of humanity. As Imam 'Ali[35] said, a human being does not comprise a small, physical body; a human being is the miniature, the most precious copy of the whole universe; the human contains the entire contents of the universe and bears witness to the Divine Being as loudly as the entire universe. With all our states, we human beings demonstrate the All-Initiating; with all aspects of our lives we exclaim that we are de-

---

34 In this translation God is always used to mean *Allah*. (Tr.)

35 Imam 'Ali is 'Ali ibn Abi Talib (606–661): One of the first four to embrace Islam and one of the greatest Companions of the Prophet Muhammad, upon him be peace and blessings, and his cousin and son-in-law, as well as the last of the four rightly-guided Caliphs. He was renowned for his profound knowledge, deep spirituality, and great courage, for his sacrifices for God's cause, and for his eloquence. (Tr.)

pendent on Him. With the outer and inner dimensions of our existence, we proclaim Him.

It is utterly unreasonable, contrary to the perceptible reality, and an unfortunate deception in the name of a scientific approach not to attribute existence, including humanity and the universe, to the Divine Being. Any existence which is not attributed to the Divine Being is groundless, meaningless, and void; any knowledge or sciences that are not connected to Him are mere delusions and illusions, any studies or analyses that do not lead to knowledge of Him are fruitless and in vain, and discussions or conversations that do not generate love of and closeness to Him in the human consciousness are useless.

It is a fact that all existent things tell us about Him with countless tongues and that the human conscience always reminds of Him with profound sensations, perceptions, and inclinations particular to it. Whenever with our physical or spiritual sensations we turn to this world of exhibition—the outer world, this book of existence, and our inner depths, we always listen to melodies about Him and are aware that we subsist by Him. God is an All-Transcendent, Peerless Existent One Who expresses Himself with everything He creates and Who makes His existence felt through our consciousness with countless tongues, and thus reminds us that He is ever present everywhere, despite His absolute freedom from time and space. All visible and invisible realms of existence loudly proclaim His Divinity and Lordship, telling us that He is worshipped because of His Being. God has absolute right to be worshipped and is rightfully besought due to His being God. For this reason, worshipping Him with praise, thank, exaltation, adoration, glorification, and devotion is our duty and His right.

As for the false deities which humans manufacture and worship, they can never be God or be substituted for Him. Humans have deified the sun, the moon, stars, seas, rivers and so on, and worshipped many false, artificial, fabricated deities, adoring thousands of fleeting, death-bound and essentially impotent things or beings. By following these and offering worship to them, human beings have actually disrespected their own selves, their spirits and their essential nature. When they have rejected them all and turned to the Absolute, True Worshipped One, they have been saved from being debased beings and discovered their own selves through the values God has bestowed on them.

Since whatever human beings have worshipped other than God has no existence by itself and owes its own existence to God, it has emerged as the product of misguided thought and has in turn disappeared with sound logic and reasoning. Misguided thought and false belief, which have appeared one after the other, have also disappeared and been forgotten one after the other, and the final say has always remained with the All-Sacred Being, Who is absolutely free from any phenomenon that can be attributed to the created, such as coming and going or appearance and disappearance. Even though some false deities have temporarily dominated the minds of a great many people and polluted them over the course of history, the human innate recognition and admission of the Creator, the True Worshipped One, which is regarded as the inherent riches and depths of human conscience, has driven away all products of illusions and delusions; as a result human beings have turned to the All-Majestic, All-High Being, Who is the Owner of the All-Beautiful Names and All-Exalted Attributes. They have turned to Him once more after every epoch of misguidance because there is no other source of power or riches that can support or satisfy the human consciousness other than Him. Anything or any being which cannot meet this great, intrinsic need of humanity can never be deserving of worship and cannot be a deity. And there is no question that such a being is not deserving of worship, which is absolutely due to the All-Sacred One called by the All-Beautiful Names and described by the All-Sacred Attributes; indeed, they cannot even be intercessors between Him and humans.

Neither Divinity nor Lordship ever admits a partner. The One Who has the absolute right to be worshipped is One and Unique.

The different events, states, and circumstances that we observe are results of the different manifestations of God's different Names and Attributes. The truth of the absolutely True One or the Ultimate Truth is free from whatever is related to quality or quantity. Moreover, He is neither a substance nor something accidental, but is absolutely free from all features and defects that are particular to corporeality. In the following poem in which he portrayed the creeds of Islam, the respected Ibrahim Haqqi of Erzurum expresses this point very beautifully:

> There is no opposite, nor peer, of my Lord in the universe;
> He is the All-Transcendent and exempt from having a form.
> He has no partners and He is free from begetting and
>   being begotten; He is Unique, having no equals—
>   these He mentions in *Suratu'l-Ikhlas*.
> He is neither a body nor a substance,
>   nor is He an accident,[36] nor of matter.
> He does not eat and drink, nor is He contained by time.
> He is absolutely free from change, alteration, and
> transformation, and from colors and having a shape as well—
>   These are His Attributes in the negative.
> He is neither in the heavens nor on the earth;
> Neither on the right nor on the left; neither before nor after;
>   He is absolutely free from any direction.
>   So He is never contained in space.

As the respected Ibrahim Haqqi says, God is neither a body nor a substance; nor is He a compound or a composite, a divisible being, or a part, nor does He have a form or shape or any other feature that is attributed to the created. He is the First, the Last, the All-Outward and the All-Inward—He is the All-Inward, more inward than anything inward in His manifestations, and the All-Outward, more outward than anything outward in His being hidden. As He has no physical contact with anything in His Acts, He is al-

---

36   Accident in philosophy means something which is added to a substance or into which a substance grows or develops over time. It is therefore not a substance. (Tr.)

so exempt from having or using any instruments in pronouncing His will or decrees.

We know Him by His hundreds of Names, such as the All-Merciful, the All-Compassionate, the All-Unique of Absolute Oneness, the Eternally Besought One, the All-Independent Single One, The All-Living, the Self-Subsisting (by Whom all subsist), the Eternally Existing One with no beginning, the All-Powerful, the All-Knowing, the All-Hearing, the All-Seeing, the All-Glorious with irresistible might, the All-Compelling, the All-Gracious and All-Beautiful, the All-Majestic, the All-Great, the All-Generous, the All-Pitying, the One Who has exclusive right to all greatness, the Divine Being, the Master, the Sovereign, the Lord, the All-Wise, the All-Speaking, the Creator, the All-Providing, and so on; we know Him by his dozens of Attributes, such as Life, Knowledge, Hearing, Seeing, Will, Power, Glory, Wisdom, Grandeur, Compelling, Being Eternally Existent with no beginning, Speech and so on. However, we can never claim that We know or that we are able to know Him perfectly; rather we must sigh with the admission: "We have not been able to know You as knowing You requires, O the All-Known," and seek refuge with the consideration: "(The admission of one's) incapacity to perceive Him is perception itself." God cannot be perceived or comprehended for He is the All-Encompassing One impossible to be comprehended. Therefore, claiming that He can be comprehended means claiming that the One Who is the All-Encompassing can be encompassed at the same time, which is clearly a contradiction. Furthermore, all the Names that are derived from certain verbs which express His Acts are not sufficient, individually or collectively, for us to be able to perceive His Essence. Logic and reason can attain knowledge of the Maker of Glory in the shade of the All-Beautiful Names only to the extent that He wills and allows this. This is all of the knowledge we can acquire concerning Him. How well the famous German poet said:

Whatever we say about Him, perception of the Essence of the All-Holy Creator is absolutely impossible. Human beings can only have some ambiguous feelings and conjectural ideas about the Divine Essence. We continuously feel and experience the existence of God both in our spirits and in nature. Therefore, what does it signify whether we know His Essence or Essential Nature or not? Even though we mention God with hundreds of Names and unique Attributes, our descriptions will fall far short of expressing the truth. Seeing that the Supreme Existence, Which we call Divinity, expresses Itself in multifarious manifestations—not only in human beings but also in all major and minor events and states in the universe and the rich, restricted bosom of nature—then to what extent can human description of such a Being be sufficient?

We must be utterly respectful of Him and self-possessed on our account. This must be the reason why both the greatest of theologians and many Sufis have preferred mentioning God with the pronoun "He." For there is limitless profundity and comprehensiveness when one avoids describing Him with any Attribute or Name. The pronoun "He," free from the restriction of any specific Attribute or Name, is a mysterious word which comprises all of His Majestic and Gracious manifestations, His All-Beautiful Names, and His Attributes of Glory. It must be because of this comprehensiveness that, provided we refer to Him by the word "He", there are those who regard "He" as being God's All-Supreme Name. I think it is more proper to regard it as the All-Supreme Name in expressing His Unity in the fullest terms possible.

* * *

When we consider the Divine Being from the viewpoint of His Uniqueness or absolute Oneness (*ahadiya*), we mean or refer to the Pure Essence without taking His Names or Attributes into consideration. When He is approached from the perspective of His Unity (*wahidiya*), He is considered together with His All-Beautiful Names and Attributes of Glory. At this point, human consciousness considers God along with all His works, Acts, Names, and Attributes; this means sensing the sphere of His Lordship.

Calling the rank of the truths of True Existence the sphere of Divinity is because this expression refers to the Necessarily Existent One as the All-Holy, Pure Essence. The All-Supreme Name *Allah* (God) is the proper title for this rank. Divinity in this sense is the title of a transcending truth that is observed on account of Its works and which is known but cannot be encompassed with Its decrees, judgments and principles. Our knowledge and perceptions concerning Divinity consist only of some of Its characteristics. This knowledge is never sufficient to attain complete knowledge of this sphere, for there are so many other exalted Attributes about Which we cannot have knowledge; complete knowledge and comprehension of Divinity requires knowing all of these Attributes and this is not possible for human beings to achieve.

From another point of view, on account of the vastness of Its manifestations, Divinity also encompasses the decrees, judgments and principles of the areas of manifestations that belong to the spheres of Divine Uniqueness or Oneness and Unity, in the sense that every thing or being is given its due. Just as all universal or particular bounties and favors pour forth from that sphere, so too are all thanks given and all acts of worship done in return for those bounties and favors directed to it.

Furthermore, Divine Uniqueness and Unity have another aspect which is related to the All-Holy, Purely Divine Essence. On account of Its mirror in which It is reflected, Divine Uniqueness or absolute Oneness has been expressed as: "God was and there was nothing else besides Him,"[37] while Divine Unity has been interpreted in the sense of *Everything is perishable (and so perishing) except His "Face." His alone is judgment and authority, and to Him you are being brought back* (28:88). While the former refers to God as eternal having no beginning, the latter refers to Him as eternal having no end. According to this approach, since the rank of Uniqueness relates to the Pure Essence, this Uniqueness has been accepted as having pre-

---

37   Related from the Prophet, upon him be peace and blessings, in Ibn Hajari'l-Asqalani, *Fathu'l-Bari*, 6:289; al-Alusi, *Ruhu'l-Ma'ani*, 9:106.

cedence over the rank of Unity, Which is considered together with the Names and Attributes. As for Divinity, It has precedence over both Uniqueness or Oneness and Unity, for It has the transcending characteristic of giving everything its due and restoring every right in the vastness of all realms of contingency, and the rank of All-Mercifulness (*ar-Rahmaniyya*), which is regarded as the horizon of the initial manifestation of all Divine Names and Attributes, has been considered as Its area of unfolding. The proper title of this rank is the All-Sacred Name the All-Merciful (*ar-Rahman*), to Which are referred the Names of the Divine Essence such as the All-Unique of Absolute Oneness, the One of Unity, the Eternally Besought One, the All-Holy, and the All-Supreme, as well as such Attributes of His like Life, Knowledge, Hearing, Seeing, Power, and Will.

The rank which encompasses God Almighty's Names, Attributes of Glory, and wise Acts has been called the sphere of Divinity on account that He is—and is accepted as—the Divine Being Who is Absolutely Deserving of Worship, while the rank which relates to the Name the Lord and draws attention to His being—and being accepted and obeyed as—the Lord has been designated as the sphere of Lordship. The statements of the Qur'an concerning both of these spheres are explicit and decisive. The Qur'an tells us to believe in God as both the One of Divinity and the One of Lordship. For example, on account of describing God Almighty with His Attributes of Perfection that are inherent in His Essence and declaring Him to be absolutely free from any attributes of defect, *Suratu'l-Ikhlas* (*Sura* 112) emphasizes the Unity of Divinity or God's being the Unique One of Divinity. While *Suratu'l-Kafirun* (*Sura* 109) pronounces that worship and adoration are particular to God exclusively, Who has no partners, rivals, or equals, and therefore emphasizes the Unity of God as the All-Worshipped One. *Suratu'l-Fatiha* (*Sura* 1) teaches and stresses both the Unity of Divinity and the Unity of God's being the All-Worshipped One and the Unity of Lordship.

If the Qur'an is studied from these aspects, it can be seen that in almost all of its chapters it teaches and emphasizes these kinds of Unity. The verses which tell us about the Names, Attributes, and Acts of God Almighty point to the "Unity of the Source of revealed knowledge" or the "Unity of Divinity," while the verses that are concerned with worshipping God Who has no partners, rivals, or equals refers to the "Unity Which demands worship and relates to will-power" or the "Unity of Lordship." The Unity of Divinity has also been interpreted as the confirmation and conviction that whatever our Prophet taught and conveyed to us is true, while the Unity of Lordship means the fulfilling of all Divine commands with the utmost sensitivity and refraining from whatever has been forbidden.

That which we have been trying to explain from the beginning consists of only some pieces of information and is in no way sufficient to express God or to be a translator of the truth of the Ultimate Truth. To date, thousands, perhaps, millions of people have tried to relate about the Essence of the Ultimate Truth and to describe Him based on their inspirations—May God reward them for their efforts! The excitement of the heart, the tears and the ink of the pen have cooperated numerous times to describe Him, but every time everything has been entrusted to the realms beyond and those further beyond, and self-possession has been preferred. What is most proper to do in this respect must be to remain content with His Own particular descriptions and instructions, saying:

> How can it be possible to describe the All-Protecting Owner!
> What is proper is not to attempt to describe Him.

If the goal and result of all these attempts to know God and to make Him known is our servanthood to Him, our love of Him, and our pleasing Him, then we should pursue these with our outer and inner senses and our faculties to try to reach our goal. He has never disappointed those who have turned to Him with love and attachment and He has never abandoned those who come to His door, or left them unrewarded.

The meaning of servanthood is explicit, and there are two aspects of "love of God." The first is loving Him, while the other is being loved by Him. Mentioning these two aspects, the Qur'an says: *God loves them, and they love Him* (5:54). That is to say, God Himself and His servants both love and are loved. This love is certainly different from the love we feel for other people. God's love of His servants is being pleased with them and favoring them with a happy end, while the believers' love of and yearning for Him is on account of His being the sole Source of all beauty, perfection, favor, as well as all gifts, bounties, and bestowals.

Loving Him and feeling attachment to Him is something from among His gifts and favors. For this reason, being a translator for others who resembled him, a saintly friend of God is reported to have said: "I thought that I knew, loved, and was seeking Him; I thought I was pursuing His good pleasure. But later I came to realize that I had been following Him in His mentioning, loving, and seeking me." That is, we know, love, mention and seek Him because He makes us know, love, mention and seek Him.

The respected Junayd al-Baghdadi expresses the same reality as follows: "I have known God by God Himself; also by God Himself or through the messages of His Messenger have I come to know the true nature of all other than Him." No matter with what Attributes He has described Himself through His inspirations and Revelations on different wavelengths, He is the All-Transcending One describable only with those Attributes, and no matter with what Names He refers to Himself, He is the All-Sacred One Who is called by those Names. Neither does His Essence or Essential Being resemble other beings, nor are His Attributes like the attributes of others. He is the First and there is none preceding Him and there is no time preceding Him; He is the Last and He makes our consciousnesses aware of eternity and His being eternal.

Saintly friends of God have advanced toward the mysteries that belong to Him through the manifestations of His Acts in the outer and inner worlds, and then through the manifestations of

His Names, and then through the manifestations of His Attributes, and then through the manifestation of His Essence. They have crowned their immaterial, invisible journey with certain kinds and degrees of visions of Him that they have attained by means of the favors and regards with which they have been honored. They have made great efforts to be able to experience manifestations of His Essence with great yearning, sometimes sighing and weeping for their pitiable states during their journey, and at others rejoicing with the breezes of nearness to and familiarity with meeting Him. They have criticized and supervised themselves in great shame before Him, paying at His door their most humble respects, and continuing their journey half-dead and half-alive. How beautiful is the following description of these experiences:

> I was ashamed of myself in the realm of love;
> turning to my body, soul, and heart, I reprimanded myself.
> I leveled to the ground the building of self on the path of love;
> O Nigari,[38] I destroyed my physical existence for the
> treasure of His love.

In a poem in his *Diwan-i Kabir*, the respected Mawlana Jalalud-Din ar-Rumi speaks about love for God as follows:

> It is incumbent upon lovers to search for the Friend. Like a wild flood, rubbing their faces against the ground and striking their heads against rocks, they should run until they reach the Friend's river. Actually, it is He Who both wills and chooses. We sometimes go toward the Friend's river babbling like a running water, and sometimes remain kept in His pitcher like standing water. And other times come when we boil like an earthenware pot on fire.

What those who know Him should do is to advance, babbling like water and weeping day and night. If those who do so are also able to read accurately whatever there is around them, they will one

---

38 Seyyid Mir Hamza Nigari was a Sufi poet from Azerbaijan. He wrote lyrical poems to express God's love. (Tr.)

day be rewarded abundantly with knowledge and love of Him and be able to realize the true purpose of their existence.

> O God! I ask You for resignation after calamity or any of Your decrees or judgments concerning me, the coolness of life after death, the pleasure of observing Your Face, and the zeal to meet You without suffering the harm of anything harmful, or any misleading intrigue and mischief. And bestow, O Lord, blessings and peace on the Inaugurator and Seal of Prophethood, on his Family and Companions, may God be pleased with them all.

METAPHYSICAL REALMS

The 'Arsh (The Supreme Throne of God)

Literally meaning an arbor, throne, roof, or the horizon of something, the word 'Arsh is the title of an elevated realm that envelops all the heavens and the earth, surrounds all systems, and which is the arena of the first manifestation of Divine will and command concerning the material and immaterial worlds. While this elevated realm is known as the 'Arsh, the area regarded as its opposite, that is, the ground, is the *farsh* (the ground, the floor). Scholars have clarified the meanings of and the differences between these two concepts by saying: "One ascends to the 'Arsh while the *Farsh* is descended to," and they have introduced the 'Arsh and *Farsh* as two opposite poles. It is also due to this approach that while the line or spirals of ascension to the 'Arsh have been described as *'arshiya* (the spiral way and curves of ascension), the line or spirals of descent are known as *farshiya* (the spiral way or curves of descent).

It would be better to describe the 'Arsh in a figurative sense as the horizon of the first manifestation of God Almighty's Power and Grandeur. For this description also refers to God's absolute freedom from matter and time. The Qur'anic statement, "God's establishing Himself on the 'Arsh" is a reality whose meaning is not clear, because acts such as settling, sitting or being established, which are particular to the created and time and space, can never be contemplated in respect of God.

Ancient astronomy considered the 'Arsh to be the ninth, most extensive firmament that surrounds all other firmaments. Astronomers also referred to the *'Arsh* as "the vastest firmament" and "the all-embracing firmament." This approach could be viewed as accurate if we take into account the knowledge of astronomy in ancient times. Modern astronomy says different things. However, we should take into consideration what the Qur'an, the accurately reported *hadiths*, and the opinions of the illustrious interpreters of the Qur'an say on the matter.

The *'Arsh* is the arena where God manifests His religious commands and His commands for creation and the operation of the universe as the Lord of the worlds; it is the luminous "area" where His Power and Grandeur are initially manifested, and it is above all the realms of creation. The mysterious nature of this realm is known by God alone, and it is a comprehensive mirror of God's Attributes of Glory and His Names that originate in His Acts. Moreover—if it is permissible to say so—this realm is the "workshop" where all living and non-living creatures are formed. It is therefore impossible for those whose scope of sight is restricted to physical eyes and therefore to the material or physical dimension of existence to comprehend this arena.

Another important topic relevant to this matter is God's establishment of Himself on the *'Arsh*. Many opinions have been put forward to explain the phrase, *Istawa ala'l-'Arsh* (25:59). First of all, the original word for self-establishing, *istawa*, literally means rising or standing upright, and the preposition used to express the direction of the act, *'ala*, means on, over, or from above. So, in addition to the meaning of rising above, this phrase also implies assuming or manifesting a position of superiority. When used for God, Who is absolutely free from having any resemblance with the created, it means God's manifesting and making known His Sovereignty and demonstrating His Power and Grandeur. The *'Arsh* is in no way related to matter, time, space, or direction, and as a result no physical, material feature or notion can be applied to it.

Secondly, as God is absolutely free from matter, from having a body, from being contained in time and space, or from being or having a substance, His self-establishing in no way resembles our sitting, settling, or being established. How can He or His Acts resemble the created or the acts of the created? This is explicitly stated in the Qur'an; while He is an all-overwhelming Power Who holds all the heavens and the earth in His grasp of Power, at the same time He is the All-Merciful and All-Compassionate Who is nearer to each human being than their jugular vein.

Thirdly, even when we speak about impotent beings like us, saying: "The king has been established on his throne," we mean that a person has become a sovereign, subdued the people, and begun to put their decrees into force. Thus, the Divine Being's absolute freedom from anything physical or corporeal makes it necessary to understand such expressions for Him in the same, figurative sense.

From the earliest days of Islam all righteous scholars have approached such expressions from this perspective and described God in the way that the respected Ibrahim Haqqi of Erzurum has described Him:

> He is neither a body nor a substance,
> nor is He an accident, nor of matter.
> He does not eat and drink, and is uncontained by time.
> He is absolutely free from change, alteration, and transformation,
> and from colors, and having a shape as well—
> These are His Attributes in the negative.
>
> ......
>
> There is no opposite, nor peer, of my Lord in the universe;
> He is the All-Transcendent and exempt from having a form.

This approach is one on which the overwhelming majority of Muslims and Muslim scholars agree, and the creed of *Ahlu's-Sunna*[39] is based on this. The earliest scholars did not argue about such subtle matters and even avoided answering questions concerning them.

---

[39] *Ahlu's-Sunna wa'l-Jama'a* is the overwhelming majority of Muslims, who follow the Prophet's and His Companions' way in thought, creed, and action. (Tr.)

When asked about God's establishing Himself on the *'Arsh*, the respected Imam Malik[40] thought for a short while and answered: "God's establishing Himself on the *'Arsh* is a reality and the acceptance of it is incumbent on us. However, its very nature is incomprehensible, and asking about it is an innovation in the Religion."[41]

However, when, in later times, certain trends of thought emerged among Muslims under the influence of foreign beliefs and philosophies, and in the face of false interpretations that imply corporeality, time, and place for God Almighty, scholars felt obliged to explain in what sense the Qur'an uses such words as *istiwa* and have tried to protect the masses against false ideas. They explain the meanings and implications of *istiwa* as follows:

- *Istiwa* alludes to the faultlessness of the order of creation and the perfection of the Sovereignty or Domination that has established and continues this order. The fact that wherever the word *istiwa* is used in the Qur'an there is also reference to this Sovereignty and Administration proves this.

- By reminding us of the usual Divine practice that is the true origin of everything and every event in the universe, the Qur'an implies that after God Almighty initially created the universe in a miraculous fashion, without applying any physical causes, He introduced the "natural" or physical causes into all events as veils before Divine Dignity and Grandeur.

- Just as all things and events come into existence with the manifestations of God's Knowledge, Power, and Will, they also subsist by His Authority and Subsisting, Which manifest themselves on and through the *'Arsh*.

- *Istiwa* also means invading and surrounding completely. Thus, with this word it is emphasized that God's Sover-

---

40   Imam Malik ibn Anas (711–795): He has born, lived, and died in Madina. He was one of the most highly respected scholars of *fiqh* (Islamic jurisprudence) and the Maliki School of Law was named after him. (Tr.)

41   al-Qurtubi, *al-Jami' li-Ahkami'l-Qur'an*, 7:219–220.

eignty is so forceful and encompassing that It can never be
compared to human sovereignty or management.

- The word *istiwa* also implies that although we are infinitely distant from God Almighty, He sees and knows everything perfectly from high above, yet is nearer to us than
  ourselves.

Reminding us of these meanings, respected scholars have tried
to protect Muslims against false notions of God in connection with
corporeality, time, and space and against falling into misguidance,
equipping us with important arguments for thinking correctly. We
are thankful to them for their sincere efforts. However, it would be
more proper to act like Imam Malik if false assertions made by misguided sects are not in question, and refer the whole of the truth to
the All-Knowing of the whole Unseen.

Some of the illustrious interpreters of the Qur'an have put forward the idea that the *'Arsh* and *Kursiyy* (the Supreme Seat) are the
same and both constitute the arena where God's Attributes of Glory and Divine Sovereignty are manifested. However, in addition to
many verifying scholars, a *hadith* mentioned in *al-Bidaya wa'n-Nihaya* by Ibnu'l-Kathir and certain other reports referred to either
the Prophet himself or his Companions show that the *'Arsh* and
Kursiyy are different arenas of manifestation. The *hadith* and reports
in question even state that the *'Arsh* is a million times larger than
the *Kursiyy*. The *'Arsh* is more encompassing in comparison to the
Kursiyy, to the same extent the *Kursiyy* is greater than the entire corporeal universe. In explaining the vastness and comprehensiveness
of the *'Arsh*, it is said that the earth, the heavens, and all elevated
realms such as Paradise, Hell, *Sidratu'l-Muntaha* and *al-Baytu'l-
Ma'mur* are encompassed by the *'Arsh*.

However, the vastness and comprehensiveness of the *'Arsh*
should not be thought of on account of itself, but on account of its
being the first arena where God Almighty's Grandeur and Sovereignty are manifested. What gives it the greatest value and makes it

unequalled among the elevated realms is that it is a mirror to overall Divine manifestation.

On account of being the primary arena where Divine Attributes of Perfection and the Names that originate in God's Acts are manifested, the *'Arsh* also has a "relative" infinitude. In one respect, all other existent things and beings and all events start and end here. Time, space, and direction are not attributable to it. It is above all such things. Therefore, the *'Arsh* encompasses both this world and the next.

Even though we are unable to perceive exactly all these or other similar realities, we believe in the existence and features of the *'Arsh* in accordance with how this arena is mentioned in the Qur'an and the accurately-reported *hadith*s; we also admit that we are unable to comprehend its true nature and refer this knowledge to the All-Knowing of the whole Unseen. When we think of the *'Arsh*, we recall the first arena of the manifestation of God's Attributes of Glory and the most luminous mirror of the Divine Names that originate in Divine Acts, and feel that we are gratified with the shadows that It sends over us from other worlds.

The *'Arsh* and the *Kursiyy* are above all other things and have a nature that transcends all time and space. However, it is not the *'Arsh* Itself which gives It this nature; since this nature is given to It by the Monarch of all eternity, Who is absolutely free from time and space, it is of a relative character.

Even though the mind always has great difficulty in comprehending such extremely subtle matters, and the sciences admit their inability to comprehend them, the spiritual intellect, which is always turned to God, somehow arrives at certain truths concerning these matters and can find many things which give it some sort of contentment. Even though humans suffer from a lack of words to express such truths, they can listen to different things from the tongue of their hearts, voice what they have grasped with praise and glorification of God, and desire to reach further and further truths. However, they should remain within the limits of their inborn capacities in the face of matters that they are unable to grasp, saying: "(The admission of one's) incapacity to perceive Him is perception itself."

In fact, a believer is a person of fairness and justice who acknowledges in advance that there may be many things that they cannot know in addition to that which they know. Even though they believe that their heart is so vast as to be able to contain worlds, they are aware that one of the most important depths of this faculty is knowing its innate deficiencies and limits of comprehension. For this reason, the heart continuously admits its inherent impotence and poverty, never removing its eyes from the All-Knowing of all that is Unseen.

Bediüzzaman Said Nursi[42] made remarkable considerations about the *'Arsh*. He wrote:

> The *'Arsh* (The Supreme Throne of God) is a combination of the Divine Names the First, the Last, the All-Outward, and the All-Inward. With respect to the Name "the All-Outward," Which forms one dimension of this combination, the Supreme Divine Throne is the envelope that encompasses all things and the universe is its contents. With respect to the Name "the All-Inward," It is like the heart of creation or the contents of the envelope, which is the universe. When viewed with respect to the Name "the First," the Supreme Divine Throne marks the start of the creation, which is indicated by: *His Supreme Throne was upon the water (a fluid)* (11:7). With respect to the Divine Name "the Last," It refers to the finality of existence, which is implied in the *hadith*: "The ceiling of Paradise is God's Supreme Throne." Therefore, due to its share in the manifestations of the four Names mentioned, we can view the *'Arsh* as a combination that embraces the universe from all directions.[43]

---

[42] Bediüzzaman Said Nursi (1877–1960): One of the greatest Muslim thinkers and scholars of the 20th century. He wrote about the truths and essentials of the Islamic faith, the meaning and importance of worship, morality, and the meaning of existence. He is very original in his approaches. *Sözler* ("The Words"), Mektubat ("The Letters"), Lem'alar ("The Gleams"), and Şualar ("The Rays") are among his famous works.

[43] *al-Mathnawi al-Nuri – Seedbed of the Light* (trans.), New Jersey, 2007, p., 150.

In addition to this consideration, Bediüzzaman puts forward another view of the *'Arsh*, which is as follows:

> In respect of His Lordship (creating, upbringing or raising, maintaining, and domination), God Almighty has made the earthly creatures an *'arsh*, (which can be viewed as the projection of the Supreme Divine Throne (*al-'Arshu'l-'A'zam* and regarded as an imperial medium for His control of the universe or for the conduction of His decrees). He has made the air an *'arsh* for His commands and will, the light an *'arsh* for His knowledge and wisdom, the water an *'arsh* for His mercy and grace, and the earth an *'arsh* for His giving of life, reviving, preserving, and providence. He circulates three of these elements around earthly creatures.[44]

If the Ka'ba is a projection or mirror of something from the realms beyond, if humankind is the polished mirror of another thing, and the physical realms are the garden or vineyard or the green house of metaphysical ones, then it is quite natural that the elements of air, water, light, and earth are mirrors of projections of some things or truths that belong to the elevated realms.

The views of Sufis about the *'Arsh* are somewhat different. Even though they do not reject the considerations of the interpreters of the Qur'an and theologians, in addition to mentioning it with such names as the Universal Intellect, the Universal Soul, and the Divine Signs of Creation, based on the verse, *His Supreme Throne was upon the water (a fluid)* (11:7), they have tended to call it the Supreme Throne of Life and the Supreme Throne of Livelihood. Sufis have also given the *'Arsh* the title the Supreme Throne of the All-Merciful because it surrounds all particles, all compounds, all the heavens, the earth, and all the realms of existence, and the title the All-Supreme Throne due to its being a mirror of the truth of the Supreme Preserved Tablet. If they have also called the heart of a believer the Supreme Throne of God, they have done so because they have viewed it (the heart) as the House of God.

---

44 *The Letters* (Trans.), New Jersey, 2007, p., 316.

This approach is widespread among the Sufis. While the respected Ibrahim Haqqi of Erzurum says,

> The heart is the House of God; purify it from
> whatever is other than Him,
> So that the All-Merciful may descend into His palace at night.

another saintly friend of God speaks as follows:

> The heart of a believer is the Supreme Throne of the All-Merciful;
> Breaking it is a sin and transgression.

THE *KURSIYY* (THE SUPREME SEAT OF GOD)

Literally meaning a special place to sit, a chair, seat, or base, *al-Kursiyy* is the title of a spiritual realm which surrounds the universe and has the position of being the base upon which the *'Arsh* (the Supreme Throne of God) stands with its "two legs." According to illustrious interpreters of the Qur'an, the *Kursiyy* is the realm where God's commands are manifested and implemented, and it has a position below the *'Arsh* (the Supreme Throne). Every thing and every being in the heavens and on the earth, all heavenly bodies, with the inhabitants of each, are encompassed by *al-Kursiyy*. For this reason, humankind, all other living and non-living beings, and all realms are strictly bound to and dependent upon the commands and laws manifested here. All the laws belong to the Owner of the *Kursiyy*, Who dominates everything; all commands issue from Him, and the care and maintenance of all of creation are the result of His being the Lord. Whatever happens and whatever characteristics there are in the entire universe are with His permission and through His creation, and He is ever aware of all of these. Whatever happens and whatever there is in the heavens or beyond the heavens—be it of a primary or secondary degree, universal or particular, originating from the soul or senses, secret or manifest—God has absolute knowledge of all at the same instant that He is aware of the feelings that occur in our hearts, the thoughts that emerge in our minds, and the blood that circulates in our veins. God sees and maintains whatever He has created, He controls and directs it, and changes and transforms it—He does all this, but, as stated in the Qur'an (2:255), He is never wearied nor does slumber or sleep seize Him. He makes the *'Arsh* a veil of the throne before His Attributes, and the *Kursiyy* a platform for His practices as the Lord. He creates what He creates, and continues the cycle of life and death, and both observes and makes observed through the *Kursiyy* that He is the All-Living and the Self-Subsistent by whom all subsist.

From the earliest interpreters of the Qur'an to contemporary ones, Muslim scholars have put forward the following views concerning the *Kursiyy*:

The *Kursiyy* is the seat of absolute authority that establishes and directs time; it is above the heavens and below the *'Arsh* and it surrounds the entire universe. It is also mentioned as the base upon which the *'Arsh* stands with its "two legs." Its building-blocks are different from the foundation stones of the corporeal realm; they are neither atoms nor electrons, nor anti-atoms or anti-electrons; they are not even ions. It is a metaphysical entity whose true nature is only known by God. It is a body but not like the bodies we know; it has a nature but this is beyond our scope of perception. It is neither a corporeal body, nor a substance, nor an accident (something additional to a substance or an essence). However, in saying this concerning the *Kursiyy*, we should bear in mind that in their absolute sense all these attributes, that is, being neither a body, nor a substance, nor an accident, and being beyond the scope of our perception, are some of God's Attributes in the negative. So using them for God in their absolute sense and for certain other beings or entities in the relative sense is a matter of belief.

The *Kursiyy* has a transcending nature, which is also viewed in connection with creation and spatial existence at the same instant that it surrounds the entire universe; this is, in the language of the interpreters of the Qur'an and using an approach close to that of the *Arsh* which, as mentioned above, was used by Bediüz-zaman, both encompassing and encompassed. As for its Owner, neither time, nor space, nor directions are in question for Him.

> He is neither in the heavens nor on the earth;
> Neither on the right nor on the left; neither before nor after;
> He is absolutely free from any direction.
> So He is never contained in space.

Ibrahim Haqqi

The *'Arsh* is His, so is the *Kursiyy*, but the All-Transcending One's relations with these are not in the forms of sitting, being established, settling, covering a space, or needing. God Almighty is never like any created thing or being. His Existence is all-sub-stantial; It is true existence and He exists by Himself. In the language of the scholars of Islam, God is the Necessarily Existent One. He has neither an opposite nor a peer, neither an equal nor a rival. The *Kursiyy* is, in a sense, the realm of the manifestation and implementation of His Commands and it is one of the truths which underlies a nature that we cannot know or comprehend; it is an elevated station that stirs up our feelings of amazement. Even though many opinions or considerations have been put forward concerning the *Kursiyy*, all of these are far from being able to describe it with its true, exact nature. They are not wrong or misleading, but it cannot be claimed that they are its exact or complete description.

The *Kursiyy* has also been viewed as the arena of the manifestation of all attributes of existence in the corporeal realm. All elevat-ed realms and all the formations, changes, alterations, transforma-tions, and instances of assuming color and shape in them occur ac-cording to the commands and rulings manifested therein. Atoms and particles revolve according to a program of Destiny by the Command and Will that is reflected from the *Kursiyy*; the stars and heavenly systems continue their existence in perfect harmony ac-cording to the principles or rulings manifested in the *Kursiyy*. The angels and spirit beings fulfill the commands of the creation and operation of the universe with their eyes fixed on the *Kursiyy*. In short, all the parts of existence, from the microcosm to the macrocosm, are made to act by the commands that issue from or through it, they preserve their accord through their connection with it, and continue to live turned to it, even though they do not abandon considering themselves in one way or another.

Those who approached the *Kursiyy* from the perspective of the astronomy of Ptolemy viewed it as "the horizon of stationary realms" in the eighth layer of the heaven, and the *'Arsh* as "the all-encompassing map" of the ninth heaven. This was what they were able to conclude according to their horizon of knowledge. According to the statements of the King of Prophets, upon him be peace and blessings, neither the *'Arsh* nor the *Kursiyy*, nor the realities concerning them are of the kind that we can approach according to our criteria; we are not able to comprehend them. Endowing them with a nature, one way or another, is beyond our capacity. In explaining the superior nature of the *Kursiyy*, the Pride of humankind, upon him be peace and blessings, says: "In relation to the *Kursiyy*, all of the worlds are like a ring cast on the desert."[45] He said so only to draw attention to the incomprehensible vastness of the *Kursiyy*, to its function as the arena of the manifestations of and as a mirror to God's commands, and to its being God's Supreme Seat, where there is never a question of God sitting or of it covering space. It therefore means that there is nothing below the *'Arsh* more sublime and grand than the *Kursiyy*.

However, some leading scholars have viewed the *'Arsh* as related to time and the *Kursiyy* as related to space, although they have considered the former with its dazzling magnificence and the latter with its grandeur. If this approach comes from relating time and space each to an established, unchanging truth, there can be no objection to this and it is not incompatible with the fact that

---

45   Ibn Hibban, *as-Sahih*, 2:77; 'Abdullah ibn Ahmed ibn Hanbal, *as-Sunna*, 1:247.

the *'Arsh* and the *Kursiyy* are both beyond time and space. Moreover, if it is indicated that the *'Arsh* and the *Kursiyy* are only relatively, not absolutely, beyond time and space, this cannot be criticized either. For absolute freedom from time and space is one of God's Attributes in the negative; nothing else can have a share from this freedom that is essentially His.

To sum up: The *Kursiyy* (God's Supreme Seat) is an arena of the manifestation of Divine Sovereignty and Rule, a special mirror of God's all-encompassing Knowledge, a spiritual means for our minds to sense His infinite Power, Will, and Knowledge, and the immaterial, luminous Seat of the All-Merciful, the All-Compassionate.

Just as the Supreme Ka'ba is called God's House as an expression of its supreme relation to God Almighty, the *'Arsh* has been called *'Arshu'r-Rahman* (The Supreme Throne of the All-Merciful) and the *Kursiyy*, *al-Kursiyyu'r-Rabbani* (The Supreme Seat of the Lord) due to the sublimity of their relations, the vastness of the meanings they contain, and the profundity of their functions. Whatever we call them, the main point is to express the grandeur of Divinity and the fact that all of the worlds, great or small, are under His absolute control and direction. If we do not approach the matter in this way, but become involved in unnecessary detail, we will overstep our limits and show disrespect to truths whose exact nature we are unable to know.

This is the *Kursiyy* that encompasses all the worlds; it is a transcending, incomprehensible Seat of the All-Merciful, the All-Compassionate. All things and their basic characteristics don the body of existence and continue to exist by Divine Command, Will, and Power, Which are manifested in it. We can neither know the exact nature of the *Kursiyy* nor grasp the Divine mysteries that are involved here. The Sufis have viewed the *Kursiyy* as the horizon of the manifestation of Divine Power, the arena for the reflection and implementation of God's injunctions and prohibitions as the Lord, and the first ground for the rise of Divine Names which originate in His Acts. Viewing it thus, the Sufis have regarded turning to that

Power in awareness of our innate impotence and poverty as the mystery of being undefeatable; they have accepted sensitivity in obedience to His injunctions and prohibitions as faithfulness to the Owner of the *Kursiyy*, and felt and experienced all of existence as the manifestations of Divine Names and the harmony they form.

SIDRATU'L-MUNTAHA (THE LOTE-TREE OF THE FURTHEST LIMIT)

Sidr literally means Arabian cherry; it also means astonishment or something that is spectacular. *Sidratu'l-Muntaha* denotes the limit, the final point, the furthest boundary of the realm of contingencies. Some have interpreted it as the final point which death-bound beings can reach. Based on certain Prophetic sayings and reports from either the Prophet, upon him be peace and blessings, or from some of his Companions, the illustrious interpreters of the Qur'an depict *Sidratu'l-Muntaha* as a blessed tree which exists to the right of God's Supreme Throne and below which flow the rivers of Paradise, which have been promised to the God-revering, pious. In order to emphasize the extent of the area it covers, our master, upon him be the most perfect of blessings and peace, says: "If a horseman were to gallop for seventy years across its shadow, he would not be able to traverse it; a single leaf of it can cover an entire nation."[46] If we use greater units of measurement to express the extent of the area it covers, we would not be exaggerating. For the *Sidra* marks the farthest boundary of the realm of creation; here it meets with the realm of the initial manifestations of Divine Commands. The realm of contingencies ends here. The branches, shoots, and leaves of the huge tree of creation, which extends in all directions, end here. Also, the views of saintly people who deepen in spirituality and those with progressive hearts who can penetrate the inner dimension of things can extend only this far. The perfected ones, who are always careful of where they put their feet and how they take each step on

---

46 at-Tabari, *Jami'u'l-Bayan*, 15:10; Ibn Kathir, *Tafsiru'l-Qur'an*, 3:20.

the way to God, stop at this boundary, without being able to take a single step further. Everyone breathes with amazement here. For what lies beyond is included in the realm of the absolute Unseen, which none other than God can know.

Another meaning of the *Sidratu'l-Muntaha* is that it signifies such a horizon of astonishment and amazement, and such a peak of passion and stupor that "there is neither space in it nor heavens and earth; and no mind can grasp this state" (Süleyman Çelebi[47]). Of the many heroes of spirituality that have emerged from humanity from the beginning of existence, none other than the Honor and Pride of Humankind, and the Peerless of Time and Space, upon him be the most perfect blessings and peace, has ever been able to rise as far as that horizon or reach that peak. Those who have reached it in their spirit have been dazzled and bewildered, being stuck in amazement and stupor. It was only the Pride of Humankind *whose sight did not swerve, nor did it go wrong; indeed, he saw one among the greatest signs of His Lord* (53:17–18). The point where he reached was *Sidratu'l-Muntaha*, which, in the words of Bediüzzaman, marks the sacred horizon between the absolutely Necessary Existence and contingency. The first and last traveler who reached this peak is the Seal of Prophethood, for whose sake the worlds were created. No one preceding him and no one succeeding him has a share in this status. How beautiful is the following couplet by Süleyman Çelebi:

> No one who came before him attained this highest status;
> No one has ever been favored with this height.

It is not possible for us to be able to imagine either the depths of Prophet Muhammad's spirituality or the things he saw and heard

---

47 Süleyman Çelebi (1351–1422) is the writer of the famous *Mawlid* (whose original name is *Wasilatu'n-Najat* ("The Means of Salvation"). He lived in Bursa, Turkey. *Mawlid,* which was composed and is widely read in Turkey on certain occasions is a long poetical history of the Prophet Muhammad's life and his matchless virtues and achievements. (Tr.)

or his experiences. We preserve our perceptions and experiences and try to understand them according to the interpretations of purified, saintly scholars.

According to some Sufis, *Sidratu'l-Muntaha* is the horizon where God Almighty favors the outer and inner worlds of His noble, distinguished servants and their spirits, souls, minds, imaginations, and original natures with the manifestations of, respectively, his Names the All-Outward and the All-Inward, and of His proper Name, His Attribute of Lordship, and His Names the All-Merciful and the Ultimate Truth. It is also the peak where God manifests His Attributes of Glory. No matter how profound and extensive emotions may be, all human information, knowledge, sensations and perceptions end at the *Sidratu'l-Muntaha* and cannot go beyond. Any claims to have gone beyond this horizon only relate to particular spiritual experiences in certain exceptional states of spiritual intoxication, and have therefore no objective value.

AL-BAYTU'L-MA'MUR (THE PROSPEROUS HOUSE)

Literally meaning the prosperous house or house of worship, *al-Baytu'l-Ma'mur* is a luminous construction above the heavens which, as stated in a *hadith,* is visited or circumambulated every day by seventy thousand angels[48]—the figure denotes multiplicity so it may actually be seventy million or more—; it is the heavenly counterpart of the Ka'ba, which exists on the same line. The angels who visit or circumambulate it once will not be able to have another turn to do so again. Both this house and the Ka'ba—God's House on the earth—are prosperous due to the deep respect which the angels, spirit beings, and many humans and jinn show them; the former is visited by the angels and spirit beings and the latter by angels, spirit beings and many humans and jinn.

Al-Baytu'l-Ma'mur is one of the sacred places by which God swears in the Qur'an (52:4). The other place of the same sacred-

---

[48] 'Abdu'r-Razzaq, *al-Musannaf,* 5:28–29; Ibn Kathir, *Tafsiru'l-Qur'an,* 3:13, 24.

ness is God's House, which, as its reflection on the earth, is the heart of the earth and the pupil of the Secure Town—Makka. The former is visited by heavenly beings, who go round it, while the latter is visited and circumambulated by those on the earth. However, it cannot be said that those who go round the former are not also moths that flit around the latter. Neither can it be said that the "heavenly" beings who live on the earth do not offer their respects to the heavenly Prosperous House. Those who visit and go round these two Houses, from which God never removes His "eyes," have special regard for the Ultimate Truth, Who returns their regard with particular compliments and favors. Those who happen to visit these blessed places are considered to be God's guests, and mean to abandon themselves in a cataract of revival. It is hoped from God that they will be saved from the causes of eternal loss, such as unbelief and misguidance. Those who reach *al-Baytu'l-Ma'mur* and visit God's House on the earth after an endeavor inspired and compelled by belief do not die misguided.

The most reliable sources provide information that *al-Baytu'l-Ma'mur* is above the heavens. Some of the Companions and respected interpreters of the Qur'an say that until the end of Prophet Noah's Messengership, upon him and our Prophet be peace, it existed where the Ka'ba is or was bound to it with a spiritual tie. However, since the people of that time did not pay it the required respect, when the Flood began God lifted it to a heavenly point on the same line as the Ka'ba. Concerning such an assertion with respect to the Unseen, we can say nothing but: "True knowledge is with God."

Some of the earlier scholars' view that *al-Baytu'l-Ma'mur* is the Ka'ba must have arisen from a confusion of the original with its projection and been based on seeing the positions where the Qur'an was sent down for the first and second times as one and the same.

There have been a few people who have put forward that the first position where the Qur'an was sent down first from the

Supreme Preserved Tablet to the heaven is *al-Baytu'l-'Izza*— the House of Honor. This must be due to the fact that since the position where the Divine Word was first embodied is regarded as a site around which sacred beings go, *al-Baytu'l-Ma'mur* has been identified with and therefore called *al-Baytu'l-'Izza*.

Some Sufis have regarded *al-Baytu'l-Ma'mur* as the heart of the heroes of "subsistence by and with God." As can also be witnessed in some approaches to the *'Arsh* and the *Kursiyy*, some Sufis have considered what is projected or relative as the original itself. In fact, *Sidratu'l-Muntaha* is related to *al-Baytu'l-Ma'mur*, and *al-Baytu'l-Ma'mur* is related to the Ka'ba, and all of these are related to the heart of a believer in varying degrees; the heart is, in one sense, both an *'Arsh* and a *Sidra* and a *Baytu'l-Ma'mur*, provided it is genuine, and not false.

> O God! O Illuminator of hearts! Illuminate our hearts with the lights of Your knowledge and pour upon us out of the knowledge of those who have proper knowledge of You! Bestow blessings and peace on our master Muhammad, the master of those who have proper knowledge of You, and on his Family and Companions, who were sincere and reached the final point of their journey to meet with You.

LAWHUN MAHFUZ (THE SUPREME PRESERVED TABLET) AND WHAT LIES BEFORE

awh is literally a board to write on, and the *Lawhun Mahfuz* is the immaterial board or tablet on which God has pre-recorded everything, material and spiritual, animate and inanimate, or it is another name for the Divine Knowledge Which relates to all of these. Since there are and can never be any changes or alterations to the *Lawhun Mahfuz*, it is called the Preserved Tablet. This immaterial realm is, as stated in *Suratu'l-Buruj* (85:21–22), the tablet where the Glorious Qur'an was identified and known before it was manifested in the Prosperous House (*al-Baytu'l-Ma'mur*), and this realm is therefore an all-comprehensive notebook in which both this world and the next, with whatever there is in each, are recorded.

> *There is nothing left unrecorded in it* (6:59).
>
> *Everything has been written down and kept in it* (36:12).
>
> *It is a register where there is the knowledge of everything that has happened and will happen* (50:4).
>
> *It is a notebook where everything that has happened and will happen to every being eternally exists* (57:22).

Truly, the Supreme Preserved Tablet is the main record in which all the worlds, whether we know them or not, and all things and events that occur in these worlds are recorded. Everything belonging to or that is from the physical and metaphysical worlds was identified and recorded on the Supreme Preserved Tablet before it was or has been sent into external existence or before it did appear or has appeared in the visible realm in accordance with its identification. Although the preordainment or predetermination of everything and their execution according to the Supreme Preserved Tablet could be perceived as some sort of fatalism or absolute determinism in existence, this is not the reality. For according to reality, "Knowledge depends on what is known," God has pre-knowledge of everything, of every action every human being will perform and how they will act in the future with their own free will, and this was written down accordingly.

Some scholars call the Supreme Preserved Tablet by other names such as the Book, the Manifest Book, the Manifest Record, the Book Kept Concealed, or the Mother Book. Since all of these have been derived from the Qur'an or accurately related Prophetic Traditions, no one can object to them. However, all of these designations are not complete translations of the exact truth of the Supreme Preserved Tablet; they designate it each from a certain aspect. What we do know about this Tablet is that, like other elevated realms, it is the title of a lofty, luminous mirror, the true nature of which we cannot completely comprehend; it is also where Divine Knowledge manifests Itself or Its contents. For this reason, some describe the Supreme Preserved Tablet as a realm where everything has been recorded in the minutest detail; the true nature of this is beyond our perception. There are many others who regard the Supreme Preserved Tablet as a title of what they call the Universal Soul, which stands above all corporeal realms. We should nevertheless point out that it is not proper to put forward about such a subtle matter personal ideas which go beyond what is set out in the Qur'an and the accurately related Prophetic Traditions. It is also an essential principle and a requirement of respect for God and self-possession before Him that we should remain silent on the matters in which there are no explicit statements from the master of creation, who is the eloquent tongue of the Unseen, upon him be peace and blessings. We should be careful and self-possessed while we are expressing information about these matters and not forget to refer the exact knowledge to God, saying: "God knows best." Also, we should refer any matters about which we have no true knowledge to those who have knowledge of them or we should keep silent in acknowledgment of our ignorance about them.

Another tablet mentioned by scholars in addition to the Supreme Preserved Tablet is the Tablet of Effacement and Confirmation, which is indicated in the following verse: *God effaces what He wills, and He confirms and establishes (what He wills): with Him is the Mother Book* (13:39). It would be useful to say some things about this tablet here.

As manifestations of His perfect Wisdom, God Almighty makes changes or annulments in His laws, that is, in those of the Religion, as well as in those of the creation and operation of the universe; He transforms these laws, reforms them or casts them into different molds. He makes alterations in systems, and on the earth, and in the social atmosphere, and He destroys some people to replace them with others. He exalts and honors whomever He wills and abases whomever He wills; He makes whomever He wills laugh and makes whomever He wills weep. Through His all-overwhelming Power, He presents all the worlds, including the earth, to the views of observers with the manifestations of His Majesty and Grace as mirrors of the Tablet of Effacement and Confirmation. Similar to His disposals in His laws of the creation and operation of the universe, God abrogates some of His religious laws to replace them with new ones; for example, He made His messages known to people through the Scripture He sent to Prophet Noah, which took the place of that which He had given to Prophet Adam, and at another time He conveyed His decrees through the Revelation He sent to Prophet Abraham upon them be peace. Taking whatever He wills from the earlier Scriptures and combining them with new additions, God gave a new Book to Prophet Moses, upon him be peace. After some time He introduced a new depth in His messages and gave Prophet David, upon him be peace, the Psalms, in which He pronounced His commands once more. Through the Gospel, God manifested a profound spirituality different from what was found in the Torah and He gave the glad tiding of Prophet Ahmad (Muhammad) through the tongue of the Messiah, alluding that the time was about to come when all the changes God had made up to that time were about to come to an end. That time arrived and God made the most illustrious person happy with the most meaningful of glad tidings through His glorious declaration, *This day I have perfected for you your Religion (with all its rules, commandments and universality), completed My favor upon you, and have been pleased to assign for you Islam as religion* (5:3).

Like the ecosystem, which has undergone changes according to the Divine laws that established and organized it before it took on its present form, the Religion—a set of certain Divine commands and prohibitions—and the religious life underwent certain changes throughout history according to the time and conditions; both evolved until they were perfected through the Messengership of the master of creation, upon him be peace and blessings. In what way and according to what apparent laws that serve as veils before Divine practices all these changes and developments occur, it is clear that every thing and every event mirrors acts or instances of confirmation and effacement. From the very instant things and events became familiar with external existence, they have continuously been located within cycles of confirmation and effacement. The instances of coming into existence are followed by deaths; the instances of coming one by one are followed by instances of going one after the other. Instances of assuming colors are followed by instances of fading away and so too are the instances of happiness and rejoicing followed by sighs and mourning. Writing and drawing are followed by effacement and change. Even though the laws and rules have remained established with their relative truths, confirmation and effacement, which can be regarded as underlying the reality of time, have never failed to continue.

Neither the earth nor any being or object has ever been able to remove itself from this universal tide, these continuous acts of destruction and survival. The bright colors of yesterday have faded away or turned yellow; the species of yesterday have been replaced by new ones, and the ruling peoples of yesterday have changed places with others. New societies have appeared in the place of the cultures and civilizations of yesterday and a different religious life has taken the place of the one that existed yesterday. The same is true for the changes, alterations, and transformations in individual, social, economic, cultural, and political life.

As believers, we are sometimes vigorous and sometimes sluggish, sometimes determined and resolute and sometimes unsure and hesitant; sometimes we are polluted by sins and sometimes we stand at the door of the Ultimate Truth repentant and remorseful. Sometimes we are so full of faith that we can challenge the entire world, while at other times we are so wearied and feeble that we only stand in fear and trembling before any event. Just as the moments when we are taken beyond the worlds by our belief and enthusiasm are not few, neither are the inauspicious moments when we drown in a mere drop of water. There are days when we gallop like unflagging horses on the path of the Ultimate Truth, but there are weeks and months when we fall tired and exhausted. Every state of us is a live projection or reflection of certain scenes on the Tablet of Divine Destiny and Decree and every attitude we adopt contains certain pictures from the Tablet of Effacement and Confirmation.

All these changes, alterations, and transformations are reflections from the Tablet of Effacement and Confirmation, which is reproduced from the Supreme Preserved Tablet, also known as the Manifest Record. The Tablet of Effacement and Confirmation is characterized by change and transformation and manifests itself through different colors and designs.

From another point of view, the Supreme Preserved Tablet, also called the Mother Book or the Manifest Record, is the origin, start, foundation, and plan of everything; it is a book or record that is itself unchanging but which contains the principles of every change and encompasses the beginning, the end, the cause, and the effect all at the same instant. It is a unique identification by the Divine Being, a spiritual register or an all-encompassing record on the lines of which everything and every event is recorded with the particular identity of each. All the Divine laws responsible for the creation and operation of the universe and for every event in the universe from the beginning to the end, all Divine laws of religion from the time of Adam to the end of time, all things and beings with all the moments of their lives, and all events with their beginning and end and all their causes and results are contained on this Tablet. This is the Supreme Preserved Tablet, but it is not possible for us to say anything definite about its true nature or identity.

Here I would like to relate Bediüzzaman's somewhat different considerations concerning the Supreme Preserve Tablet and the Tablet of Effacement and Confirmation. What follows is a summary of his views:

> The Qur'an mentions the Manifest Record and the Manifest Book in several places. Some interpreters (of the Qur'an) consider these to be identical in meaning, while others say they have different meanings and connotations. The explanations of their true nature differ, but all are in agreement that both describe Divine Knowledge. However, through the enlightenment of the Qur'an, I have arrived at the following conviction:
>
> The Manifest Record, which relates more to the World of the Unseen than to the visible, material world, expresses one aspect of Divine Knowledge and Commands. That is, it relates more to the past and future than to the present. It is a book of Divine Destiny that contains the origins, roots, and seeds of things, rather than their flourishing forms in their visible existence.
>
> By growing into their full bodies with perfect order and art, the origins, sources, and roots of things show that they are arranged according to a book of the principles contained in the Divine Knowledge. Likewise, the seeds, results, and fruits of things, which contain the tables-of-contents and programs of beings that will come into existence, demonstrate that each is a miniature register of the Divine Commands. For example, it can be said that a seed is the miniature embodiment of the

program and table of its contents according to which a tree may be formed and of the Divine principles or commands which determine this program and table. In short, the Manifest Record is a table-of-contents and program of the Tree of Creation as a whole, which spreads its branches through the past and future and the World of the Unseen. In this sense, it is a book of Divine Destiny or a register of its principles. By means of the dictates and demands of these principles, atoms are used and managed for things to come into existence and to continue their existence.

As for the Manifest Book, it relates more to the visible, material world than to the World of the Unseen, and more to the present than to the past and future. It expresses Divine Power and Will rather than Divine Knowledge and Commands. If the Manifest Record is the book of Divine Destiny, the Manifest Book is the book of Divine Power. In other words, the perfect art and orderliness in everything's essence and existence, as well as its attributes and functions, show that everything is made to exist in accordance with the laws of an effective, all-penetrating Will and the principles of a perfect, absolute Power. Everything is specifically formed and given an appointed measure and particular shape. This shows that Divine Power and Will have a universal, comprehensive register of laws, a great book, according to which a particular existence and form are determined for each entity.

Curiously, although the people of neglect, misguidance, and corrupt philosophy are aware of the existence of the Supreme Preserved Tablet (*Lawhun Mahfuz*) of the Creative Power and the manifestations and reflections of the Manifest Book of Divine Wisdom and Will on things, they name it "nature," thus making it completely meaningless. In sum, through the dictates of the Manifest Record, that is, through the decrees and instructions of the Divine Destiny, Divine Power uses atoms to create or manifest the chain of beings, each link of which is His sign, on the metaphorical or "ideal" page of time, which is called the Tablet of Effacement and Confirmation. Thus, atoms are set to move so that beings may be transferred from the World of the Unseen to the material, visible world, from (the Realm of) Knowledge to the (Realm of) Power.

> The Tablet of Effacement and Confirmation is the tablet on which beings are inscribed and then removed or effaced according to their origins in, or the dictates of, the Supreme Preserved Tablet. Therefore, it displays continuous change. The Tablet of Effacement and Confirmation constitutes the essence of time. Time, a mighty river that flows through existence, has its essence in the Divine Power's inscription of beings and in the ink It uses. Only God knows the Unseen.[49]

The scholars of Sufism have usually viewed the Supreme Preserved Tablet as the start, origin, and central point of the sphere of existence and as the title of what they call "the Universal, Speaking Soul," which was created after the Most Exalted Pen. It is the first center of the identification of all of creation on the horizon of Knowledge by the Knowledge Itself. It is a Divine light which was manifested in the same relationship with the Universal Intellect as Eve had with Adam—this is such an all-encompassing Divine light that all the worlds are but an extended shadow of this light, dependent on Divine Power; all of the Divine religious laws are an illuminating ray of it issued from Divine Speech, and the Law Prophet Muhammad, upon him be the most perfect blessings, brought is the continuous radiance of it. These approaches of Sufi scholars mark some depths of the Supreme Preserved Tablet.

It has also been called the Tablet of Light on account of its relation to Divine Unity and absolute Glory, and the Tablet of Divinity due to its being the first mirror to Divine Being's Attributes of Perfection and reflecting Divine mysteries; it is known as the Tablet of Judgment owing to its being the origin of Divine orders and prohibitions, and the Tablet of Wisdom because of its being a source from which gifts and blessings pour into hearts and spirits. Each of these designations marks the growth or flourishing of a different mystery of Divine Lordship. Since everything depends on and ends in it, it manifests Divine Unity. God's Attributes of Perfection rise in it and surround all material and immaterial worlds.

---

[49] *The Words* (trans.), New Jersey, 2007, p., 566.

Hearts revive through the lights that emanate from it and become its mirrors. Spirits are awakened by means of the rays that diffuse from it and humans tend to worship its Owner. It is due to this last aspect that the Sufis have called it the Tablet of Devoted Servanthood and have stressed that Divine purposes and demands are intertwined there. The dignity of belief in Divine Unity, sincere devotion or servanthood, the truth of submission to God and perfect reliance on Him, the feeling of resignation to His decrees and judgments, and the considerations of fear and awe are the fruits of this horizon. All of these have been regarded as sweet water that gushes forth from this depth.

It cannot be said that all these meanings attributed by some Sufis to the Supreme Preserved Tablet have been derived from the Qur'an or the accurately related Prophetic Traditions. However, no one can object to the fact that the consciences that have turned to Him completely with their mental faculties and profound hearts have been honored with certain favors and gifts. Thousands of people have so far been favored with so many gifts and honored with exceptional heavenly repasts by means of their turning to Him completely and concentrating on Him. Provided they are not incompatible with the spirit of the Religion, it cannot be harmful to accept such considerations and interpretations as special gifts and favors that have been sent to them.

Some Sufis have regarded the tablets (meanings) in question, which seem to be unfolding aspects of the truth of the Supreme Preserved Tablet, as the Tablet of Moses or the Ten Commandments. This approach may be acceptable if it refers to a particular aspect of the universal truth of the Manifest Record; otherwise it restricts a vast, universal truth to a single people. The truth of the Supreme Preserved Tablet is the blessed title of an essential truth which embraces all times and places through eternity and reflects its own color and design on everything. For this reason, every sort of restriction is incompatible with its all-encompassing nature.

Our Lord, take us not to task if we forget or make mistakes! Do not disgrace us either in this world or in the Hereafter! Bestow on us favors manifest and hidden, and make our souls contented with You and "reunion" with You, resigned to whatever You judge for us and satisfied with Your offerings; bestow blessing and peace on the most honorable of Your creation, our master Muhammad, and on his pure Family and excellent Companions.

(*TA 'AYYUNAT*) IDENTIFICATIONS
AND WHAT LIES BEFORE

L iterally meaning coming forward, emerging and being made specific, in Sufi terminology *ta'ayyun* means that the different natures or different essential characteristics inherent in the Divine Being manifest themselves with different wavelengths and ranks and infinitely expand in the All-Existent, the All-Life, and the All-Knowledge beyond all modalities of quality. In the rank of absolute Necessity, *ta'ayyun* is called the First Manifestation, the All-Sacred Emergence, the Breath of Mercy, while in the rank of contingency it is known as the First Intellect, the Most Exalted Pen, the First Light, and the Truth of Muhammad or the Muhammadan Truth.

Even though there is nothing explicit in the Qur'an or the Prophetic Traditions concerning *ta'ayyun*, it can be said that the statements regarding elevated, metaphysical realms such as Divine Knowledge, the Supreme Preserved Tablet of Truth, and the Manifest Record also relate to the rank of *ta'ayyun* (identification) either by allusion or implication. Some Sufis such as Muhyid-Din Ibnu'l-'Arabi and as-Suhrawardi, as well as Mulla Jami', who was a great lover of God, and Ismail Haqqi Bursavi from among the Ottoman Sufi scholars and authors, have seen the things we perceive with our five senses as the manifestations of the ideal forms in the Realm of Ideal Forms or Representations.[50] They have, in turn, perceived the ideal forms or pictures as mirrors of spiritual substances, the spiri-

---

50 Please refer to the explanations concerning this realm in the 3rd volume of *Emerald Hills of the Heart*.

tual substances as the growths of the identifications in Knowledge, the identifications in Knowledge as reflections of the archetypes (previously discussed),[51] the archetypes as the manifestations of Divine Names (to be discussed later),[52] the Divine Names as scenes or spectacles of the Divine Attributes of Glory, and the Divine Attributes of Glory as the descriptive designations of the Pure Divine Being. However, the approaches of Imam ar-Rabbani[53] and his followers are different and worthy of discussion.

The things and abstract natures which are not included in the identifications in question and which we can designate as "contingent truths" do not share this rank of identification. On account of their existence in Divine Knowledge and the places that have been assigned to them on the Supreme Preserved Tablet of Truth—these places are turned to the Divine Names in respect of the ability and the capacity that have been bestowed on them—they proceed to the different ranks of identification through the messages that emanate from the Divine Attributes of Glory and through the manifestations of Divine Names; from here they proceed to the archetypes, and then to the external existence on the workbench of the Divine Will and Power, thus continuing to be mirrors (to all abstract Divine truths).

All the faces that are turned to the Divine Names look to the All-Sacred One, Who is called by these Names, from behind veils. In this rank or step, the Name *al-Bari* (the All-Holy Creator) is the first "intercessor" or the first addressee of the All-Glorified's Will.

---

51 Please refer to matters discussed in connection with the spirit in the 3rd volume of *Emerald Hills of the Heart*.

52 The issue of archetypes was also discussed previously in the 3rd volume of *Emerald Hills of the Heart*. (Tr.)

53 Imam Rabbani, Ahmad Faruq al-Sarhandi (d. 1624): The "reviver of the second millennium." Born in Sarhand (India) and well-versed in Islamic sciences, he removed many corrupt elements from Sufism. He taught Shah Alamgir or Awrangzeb (d. 1707), who had a committee of scholars prepare the most comprehensive compendium of Hanafi Law. His work, *The Letters* are very famous and widely known throughout the Muslim World. (Tr.)

This blessed Name manifests Itself in connection with the glorious Name the All-Powerful, Whose "eye" is, in turn, fixed on the Name the All-Willing. This supreme Name is turned to the all-encompassing Name the All-Knowing. All things at all the ranks of identification, which have their existence in Divine Knowledge, are abstract pictures, meanings, or the immaterial substances in the all-encompassing design, which is the infinite arena of the manifestation of the Divine Attribute of Knowledge. Each member of creation in this design passes through different steps of identification to rise to their potential level of perfection.

Along the lines of the identification discussed above, the abstract truths that exist in the encompassing area of Divine Knowledge beyond all modalities of quality and quantity and beyond all forms of comparison, proceed in extraordinary measures toward their fully developed forms in the direction established by the Command and Will of the Lord of the worlds and in dependency upon their relative realities and first compacted identification. The All-Willing is God; therefore, Will is His Attribute and the measures belong to Him. The All-Developing is an Attribute of Glory belonging to the Lord of the worlds, and developing and unfolding originate in His being the Lord. He is the unique owner of the reality, "God does whatever He wills and decrees however He wills." As stated in the verse, *He directs all affairs (as the sole Ruler of creation), and He sets out in detail the signs and proofs of the truth* (13:2), determining, directing, developing, and unfolding belong to Him exclusively.

On account of His Divine Essence, He is the All-Unique of absolute Oneness, and with respect to His Attributes, He is the One of absolute Unity. Behind all the worlds of multiplicity, in their origination and arrangement, and at all the ranks or degrees of identification, the manifestations of His Uniqueness and Unity are observable. Divine Uniqueness, which we can also designate as the Essential Uniqueness of the Divine Being, or as Absorption within Absorption, or the Truth of Truths, is the rank to which all of the Divine Attributes and Names are referred; the one favored with perfect knowledge of God who has spiritually experienced this rank is aware of nothing other than Him. As for the rank of Divine Unity, which is also called the Rank of Absorption, this is a Divine door opening onto the manifestations that extend toward multiplicity, and this is a horizon of mysteries where the compacted essences begin developing and unfolding. If we view the first of these two ranks in the name of identifications as a table of contents or a seed, I hope it would not be harmful to see the other as a book, or as a tree, or as the source of all the worlds that have come into existence.

Some have understood the first identification as the manifestation of the Divine Being in His Own Essence and have designated this identification, concerning which any Attribute or Name cannot be in question, as the All-Sacred Uniqueness. This approach marks the initial truth that there is nothing other than the Divine Being. The Prophetic Tradition, "God was and there was nothing else besides Him,"[54] expresses this truth, which points to the Divine Essence Himself. Actually, it is difficult to make any interpretation concerning the nature of identification in this rank where nothing other than the Divine Essence can be mentioned.

The appearance of the Divine Uniqueness as a manifestation on the horizon of Divine Unity beyond description or any modality of quality is the peak at which identifications begin. The transcending, imperceptible "identification as Existence" and "identification as Knowledge" can only be imagined as ambiguous, imperceptible natures or programs after this first or highest rank; they are beyond all modalities of quality, and any capacity of perception, and beyond all comparisons. In this second rank of identification, the spirit, archetypes, and "ideal" existences are forged to creation or external existence on the workbench of Divine Will and Power under the guardianship of the Divine Names upon which

---

[54] See footnote 37. (Tr.)

they depend and in accordance with the plans and projects that are recorded on the Supreme Preserved Tablet of Truth.

The Most Exalted Pen, dependent on the First Intellect, which is regarded as the first identification from another perspective or in the rank of contingency, is the means of the inscription of Divine commands of creation, and the "words, sentences, and paragraphs" of the Divine pattern of creation which are projected on the tablet of the essential natures are the results of its development, expansion, and elaboration. According to the approach of Bediüzzaman: "If this universe is to be viewed as a macro book, the light of our Prophet, upon him be the most perfect blessings and peace, is the ink of the Pen of the Author of that book; if the universe is considered as a tree, his light is both its seed and its most illustrious fruit. If existence is regarded as a macro living being, his light is its spirit."[55] For this reason, with respect to creation, our Prophet is "everything" both as a seed at the beginning of contingent existence and its most illustrious fruit.

Since it would imply an attribution of temporal or accidental occurrences and changes to the Divine Essence, no identification has been accepted with respect to the Divine Essence. For it is not permissible to attribute any temporal or accidental occurrences to the Eternal Being Who has no beginning and is uncontained by time. Although everything is a manifestation of His Existence, Life, and Knowledge, neither the images in "mirrors" nor the forms on "screens" can ever be He.

As for identifications in the form of creation, they exist and subsist by following one another in dependence on their sources. We can liken this to a straight line which moves or is spun continuously and at great speed, thus appearing as a flat surface.

Some have seen the mysteries of the rank of Divinity in identifications in Knowledge and the secrets of creation in the identifications perceptible by the intellect. They have discerned the Mercy

---

55 *al-Mathnawi al-Nuri – Seedbed of the Light* (trans.), New Jersey, 2007, p., 169.

at the beginning of the identification of Divinity and emphatically expressed that the creation of the universe is based on Mercy. According to those who think thus, Mercy is essential in creation; everything comes from It and returns to It. Things such as misguidance, wrath, unbelief, and ingratitude are accidental and deviances caused by the misuse of free will.

All existent things and/or beings have passed through the spiritual, ideal, intermediary, and external stages of existence through identifications of Knowledge and as a consequence, the seed has grown into a massive tree. The first identification was, in one respect (in the rank of contingency), manifested as the truth of humanity. Prophet Adam and his progeny have formed the most important link of this process with their "bright" and "dark" aspects. The master of creation, upon him be peace and blessings, who, despite coming later in time, outstripped and excelled all others, and his believing and devoted Community have been exalted with the most perfect of statures and the distinction of being the nearest to the realization of the Divine purposes of identifications. For the master of creation is the most comprehensive and brightest mirror of Divine truths and the central point of the first, last, outward, and inward dimensions of existence, which were appointed by God's being the First, the Last, the All-Outward, and the All-Inward.

It is possible to express these subtle points in a more understandable way as follows:

Identification has been considered within different Divine and creational frameworks. The beginning of Divine identification is God's Attribute of Knowledge, and its end is God's limitless words of Glory, which have different degrees. The first of the creative identifications is the spirit of Muhammad, upon him be peace and blessings, and its finality is the tree of all of humankind with all its branches including those of the Prophets and Messengers, and the garden of the entire existence. Those who have interpreted the Divine identification as the Hidden Treasure have designated it as the Most Inward of the Inward, and considered it in the context of *the eyes do not comprehend Him* (6:103), and the basic principle, "(Admission of one's) incapacity to perceive Him is perception itself."

The spirit of Muhammad, upon him be peace and blessings, is a pure substance of light free from matter and the Universal Intellect, which has perfect knowledge of the All-Glorious Creator. The Prophetic saying: "The first thing which God created is intellect,"[56] indicates this depth; some call it the Supreme or Most Superior Spirit. For in one respect, the everlasting Life of the Divine Essence first expanded in that mirror in the universe, and as declared in the *hadith qudsi*: "But for your spiritual existence, (which apparently consists in a single entity in respect of its relation with Divine Existence and in a body in the external realm, but which is so broad as to contain the entire universe as being the seed of the entire creation in Divine Knowledge, and which is regarded as the cause of the creation of the universe,) I would not have created the worlds,"[57] Prophet Muhammad, upon him be peace and blessings, is the purpose for the creation of the universe. Out of His Will of Glory, God Almighty bestowed on that illustrious being His mysterious key to the first door, or initial development, of the Hidden Treasure, and made Him the center on which His love is focused. Therefore, as stated in the following couplet of the respected Qudsi:

> All things have come into existence from
> "I was a Hidden Treasure,"
> The ocean of love has produced waves
> through the breeze of His love.

the mysteries of Divinity were known through Prophet Muhammad to the extent they could be known, and the expansion and unfolding of the mysteries of His Lordship were witnessed through

---

56   ad-Daylami, *al-Musnad*, 1:13; Ibn Hajari'l-Asqalani, *Fathu'l-Bari*, 6:289.

57   'Alliyyu'y-Qari, al-Masnu', 150; al-Asraru'l-Marfu'a, 1:385; for variant wordings of this *hadith qudsi*, see al-Hakim, *al-Mustadrak*, 2:672; al-Bayhaqi, *Dalailu'n-Nubuwwa*, 5:489.

him. God Almighty, Who knows and sees His Own Essence and observes His Essence in Himself, has also made Himself known or opened a blessed door to be known by everybody through our master's brightest mirror. How well Süleyman Çelebi speaks:

> I have made your being a mirror to My Being,
> I have also inscribed your Name together with Mine.
>   ....
> Turn to the world and call them to Me,
> So that they may come and see My Face.

Both through his first identification as a seed or nucleus marking the beginning of creation and through his growth and expansion like the *Touba* tree of Paradise in his earthly life, Prophet Muhammad was honored with being chosen, in the words of Bediüzzaman, to be the ink in the Pen of the Author of this book of the universe, and he was distinguished with developing into a most fruitful blessed tree and being the source of dazzling and magnificent "gardens" and "orchards." Prophet Muhammad, upon him be peace and blessings, is the basic meaning of the poem of creation, the central embroidery in the lacework of existence, and the most meaningful part or rhyme of the poetic composition of Prophethood and Messengership, reflecting its spirit and contents. The heavenly Revelation manifested through him is the most comprehensive voice of the heavens and earth; his happy Ascension, which combines the nearest and farthest points of the universe, is an untouched gift of the Garden of Divinity to him in return for his magnificent position and attainments and a reward from the All-Munificent, the All-Generous—a reward that no one else has ever been or will ever be favored with. Just as through the rays of the Revelation impressive of infinitude, Prophet Muhammad felt and experienced transcendent mysteries beyond human considerations, which eyes have never seen nor ears have ever heard, so through his blessed Ascension he observed the entire existence from beginning to end and enjoyed exceptional experiences in the name of the Divine Essence, Attributes, and Names.

His experiences were of an exceptional profundity, and making God known by others was the expression of his unparalleled appreciation; his ability to guide natures of sufficient capacity to their perfection was an incomparable success. People of perfection have been able to recognize true perfection and perfectibility through him and the peaks that seem to be insurmountable have been surmounted through him. The respected Aziz Mahmud Hudai[58] says:

> All perfected ones have attained perfection through your light;
> Your existence is the perfect mirror of God, O God's Messenger.

This means that God's Messenger, upon him be peace and blessings, was exceptionally favored with complete manifestations of Divine Names and Attributes of Glory.

According to the respected Imam ar-Rabbani, the first identification is that of Existence or Existential Identification, and all identifications of Names and Attributes depend on this. From another different perspective, the All-Sacred Divine Essence and Attributes seem to be of the same rank. For this reason, to arrive decisively at the conclusion that the Attributes are different or other than the Essence would not be correct. For although the Attributes are particular and indispensable to the Divine Essence, and mark the unfolding of His Perfection, neither the Attributes themselves nor their unfolding or relation with the Essence should ever be thought of in terms of the created beings and their attributes. What is appropriate in viewing this matter, which is beyond our comprehension, is being content with the relevant statement of God and His Messenger.

---

58 Aziz Mahmud Hudai (1541–1648) was among the most famous saints in the 17th century Ottoman Turkey. He was a judge in Bursa for some time. Then he moved to Istanbul as a preacher and spiritual teacher. He has a *Diwan* containing his poems. (Tr.)

Since God's eternal Knowledge relates to everything in the existing realms and the realms of non-existence within the framework of certain identifications, billions times billions of spiritual, ideal, intermediary, and corporeal forms come into being. But this would never mean that the Divine Essence and Attributes are changeable. Both the Essence and Attributes are of the unchangeable rank, and all the changes and different states and natures belong to their mirrors.

The respected Imam (ar-Rabbani) has a different approach to the beginning of the ranks of identification. According to him, the beginning of Prophet Abraham's identification is in one respect the first identification; its being the first rank of identification is on account of identification in regard to existence or existential identification in the non-Divine realm. At the central point of this identification is the beginning of the master of creation's identification. In other, clearer words, the Truth of Muhammad is a comprehensive truth and is like the nucleus of the first identification. The truths of not only all other Prophets and Messengers but also the angels, upon them all be blessings and peace, are shadows of that central point or nucleus and Divine inscription. The Prophetic sayings: "The first thing which God created is my light,"[59] and "God created me out of His Own Light and believers out of my light,"[60] mark or refer to this reality.

In addition, that most supreme light among the creation is the most reliable and trustworthy means and guide of reaching the Ultimate Truth, while the other Prophets are each an extended shadow that revolve around the axis of this guide. The Truth of Ahmad (embodied by Prophet Muhammad before his external existence in the world), in one respect, and the undying Truth of Muhammad, upon him be peace and blessings to the fullness of the heavens and the earth, is a transcendent truth which stands at the intersection of Absolute Necessity and contingency, as referred to in *So he was (so near that there was left only the distance*

---

[59]   al-Alusi, *Ruhu'l-Ma'ani*, 8:71; al-'Ajluni, *Kashfu'l-Khafa'*, 311–312.

[60]   al-'Ajluni, *ibid.*, 1:311.

between) the strings of two bows (put adjacent to each other), or even nearer (than that) (53:9). The identification of this truth is identification in Knowledge and is characterized by love. It was the reason or purpose of the existence of the universe, and the fact that it is identification in Knowledge marks the beginning of all other identifications and manifestations.

Muhyid-Din ibnu'l-'Arabi and those who follow his way of thought have regarded the first identification, which they have viewed as the Truth of Muhammad, as the summation of Divine Attributes of Glory on the horizon of Knowledge. As mentioned before, Imam ar-Rabbani and those who think like him (whether they came before or after him) have viewed the first identification as identification with respect to Existence and stressed that its central point is the Truth of Muhammad, upon him be the most perfect blessings and peace. They have therefore argued that it is not possible to think of the creation without considering God's all-sacred, transcendent love of Himself, and the identification that is affiliated with Existence. The Truth of Muhammad is the origin of all identifications in the non-Divine realm, or it is of central character, while all other spheres of identification around it are shadows in relation to that supreme light. All spiritual, ideal, substantial, accidental, and corporeal identifications are like lamps which receive their light or are lit from it. How well Imam Busiri[61] speaks:

> All the miracles the other noble Prophets worked,
> Were only things that reached them from his light.
> He is the sun of virtues, while the others were the stars,
> Which shine only at night (when there is no sun).

Prophet Muhammad, upon him be peace and blessings, was the ultimate purpose for the existence of the universe and the only

---

61 Muhammad ibn Sa'id al-Busiri (Busayri) (1212–1296) was born and mainly lived in Egypt. He studied both Islamic sciences and language and literature. He is known primarily for his *Qasidatu'l-Burda* ("The Eulogy of the Cloak"), which he wrote in praise of our Prophet Muhammad, upon him be peace and blessings. (Tr.)

existent being who was talked about in the realms beyond. He was the first rose which bloomed on the breast of non-existence in the non-Divine realm. He was the nightingale whose voice resonated in the garden of the universe. He was the perfect leader and the unique guide in all aspects of life, and he was the fine lace that lay over the form of creation prior to ethereal existence.

> O God! Bestow blessings and peace on our master Muhammad; he was the first of the Prophets, whom You created out of Your Light; and he was the last of the pure, godly and those nearest to You, whom You created out of Your effulgence. He was confirmed by miracles and chosen for Messengership. And bestow Your blessings and peace also on his Family and Companions, who explained what he brought from You, and set forth its proofs, and publicized it.

GOD'S ATTRIBUTES OF GLORY

According to the religious methodology or the basic principles of religion, God's Attributes consist of certain transcending and blessed concepts—whose transcendence and blessedness come from the Being Whom they describe; these describe God Almighty and are, in one sense, regarded as the veils of the Divine Essence. These blessed concepts, mentioned as the Attributes of the Divine Being, are either in the form of nouns, infinitives, adverbs, or adjectives.

As a mental consideration, there are realms both before and beyond the Attributes of Glory. All the acts and phenomena in both the material and immaterial realms are manifestations of Divine Names; these Names originate from the Attributes. The Attributes are based on the Essential Qualities or Characteristics of the Divine Being, of Which perhaps only the people of spiritual unveiling and vision can be aware, and the Essential Qualities or Characteristics of the Divine Beings, as well as the Attributes, Names, and Acts ultimately end in the Divine Essence. Even though the true nature of the Names and Attributes and the Essential Characteristics are unknown to us, there is a subtle difference between the Names and Attributes. The words that describe God the All-Supreme in the form of adjectives, such as the All-Living, the Self-Subsistent, the All-Hearing, the All-Seeing, and the All-Knowing, are Names, while the concepts used in relative to the Divine Essence have been mentioned as God's Attributes or Divine Attributes.

Among the exalted Attributes that belong to God Almighty there is nothing that implies impotence, defect, or fault. For this reason, all of the Divine Attributes of Glory have been designated as Attributes of Perfection. Therefore, believing in God Almighty, exalted is His Majesty, means believing in an All-Supreme Being Who is absolutely free from any attributes of defect and Who is only describable by the Attributes of Perfection appropriate for His All-Supreme Being.

Like His Essence, God's Attributes of Glory are eternal, having neither a beginning nor an end. Even though the attributes of all created beings, like humankind and jinn, are reflections of God's Attributes, they have both a beginning and an end and their continuance depends on Divine Attributes, each of Which is living and luminous. Neither the lives of humankind, jinn, angels, or spirit beings, nor their knowledge and will resemble God's Life, Knowledge, and Will. He has no equals, peers, rivals, or opposites both in His Essence and Attributes. As He encompasses all the things, beings, and events, whether they have come into existence or not, or have happened or not, with His all-encompassing Knowledge and with His Power and Will, He is the unique Owner and Ruler of all visible and invisible things, beings, natures, and characteristics.

Whatever we say or can say concerning the Divine Being can only be concerned with His Acts and Names, and in a sense, His Attributes. As for the All-Holy Essence, He is absolutely beyond our comprehension. For this reason, thinking or putting forward opinions about Him is something regarded as risky and it is forbidden. Declaring, *Eyes comprehend Him not, but He comprehends all eyes. He is the All-Subtle (penetrating everything no matter how small), the All-Aware* (6:103), the holy Qur'an indicates the final point to which we can go in this respect and reminds that One Who is the All-Encompassing or All-Comprehending cannot be encompassed or comprehended.

With respect to our capacity of perception, the All-Holy Essence is One Who is known with His Names and Who encompasses everything with His Attributes. This marks the farthest limit of human thought and comprehension. As for the knowledge concerning the realms beyond and the truths that lie beyond, it consists only of or can only be based on intuition, spiritual experiences, and visions. This knowledge, which is imparted only to the people of a certain level, can be regarded as the Ultimate Truth's special gift in return for faithfulness, constancy, resolution, and endeavor. Also, the truth of the matters concerning Divine Destiny and Decree, which the master of creation, upon him be peace and blessings, became aware of during his Ascension, is unfolded only for those of this same level of "sight" and "hearing."

Hearing, sight, and feeling in this corporeal world occur by means of certain causes and means, and what we experience here is the lowest level of these functions. It is God Who supplies us with the necessary means for these functions and it is He Who creates these functions as well. It is He Who creates both our eyes and ears and our sight and hearing. Therefore, all the senses and organs that comprise a human body are only veils before the Divine Power and Will and they act as screens to reflect the same; however, on account of being means, they are regarded as the performers of the acts in question. In fact, they are not the actors, but are only means and causes; it is God Who creates all human acts. Just as any sound that is emitted by God's leave from an inanimate object or animal unable to speak cannot be due to the attribute or ability of that object or animal, so too the acts of human beings and the fruits that emanate from these acts belong essentially to the Creator of all things. To explain more clearly, by way of an example, God Almighty has created the attribute of knowledge in human beings and the jinn, thus preparing the ground for their relationships with the objects to be known, guiding their attribute of knowledge to its field of learning, and enabling the objects to be known to be unfolded in it. Comparing hearing and sight to this, we can say that the Unique and Absolute One of Unity has created the senses and organs of hearing and sight, established their relationships with the brain and other relevant systems, and entrusted these functions to the relevant mechanisms. It is because of all these facts that we say that the True Knowing, Hearing, and Seeing One is He, and affirm that it is He Who knows everything, has absolute power over everything, sees everything, and hears every voice or sound. We say and affirm: "There is no one else other than the Ultimate Truth who exists by themselves, or who is their own true owner, and there is no true owner, master, or object of worship other than He both in this world and the next."

In fact, everything other than the All-Holy Divine Essence is, in one sense, something other than Him. According to the people of spiritual vision and experience, even His Attributes of Glory and All-Beautiful Names are also other than Him, although from a different perspective the Muslim theologians affirm that His Attributes are neither He nor other than Him.

Life is the most comprehensive of all the Divine Attributes of Glory. What is the most indispensable to life is the (Holy) Existence; this is followed by the Attribute of Knowledge, Which has the broadest of dimensions. Knowledge is also important in respect of Its being the beginning of our master's identification, upon him be the most perfect blessings and peace. The Attributes other than Knowledge mark the beginning of the universal identification of the other "Chosen, Best Ones (of the creation)"—the other Messengers and Prophets.

Each Attribute is the cause of the emergence of many people of universality as well as numerous ones of particularity. These are the ranks of the identification of beings of different ranks of life. That is, a particular Attribute manifests Itself on some people—like Prophets—in a universal form and gives them their particular character. So, in relation to this Attribute, those people reflect It universally and takes on a universal character. However, many other people reflect the same Attribute in a particular form by following those of universal character. Universality is, in one sense, of an original function and nature, while particularity is of a shadowy one. Those—like Prophets—whose rank of identification is of a universal nature are the foundations or originals in the axis or orbit where they are located, and the others, whose identifications are of a particular nature, are their projections and are regarded as existing under their feet, or following in their footsteps. One with a shadowy nature can, in one sense, reflect the characteristics of the original, but is never identical to it. The narrowness in observation, the excessive good opinion of the particulars by their followers, and their concentration on them may cause a particular or one of a shadowy nature to be confused with the universal or the original. Those who cannot view matters with the eyes of the Shari'a may be deceived and regard, for example, a shadow which moves around the orbit of the Messiah as the Messiah himself. In addition, purposeful and planned claims by the many who attribute themselves great ranks due to such confusion and deception are not few—may God preserve us from such deceptions and claims.

Some have expressed their views of the original and shadow with statements that a certain person is under the feet or following in the footsteps of the master of creation, upon him be peace and blessings, or that another person is under the feet or following in the footsteps of Prophet Moses, upon him and our Prophet be peace, or that yet another is under the feet or following in the footsteps of Prophet Jesus, upon him and our Prophet be peace. Through the ways of spiritual progress and spiritual journey, those of shadowy nature and rank can benefit from the special blessings that arrive at the orbit or axis of the originals. Therefore, the particulars can assume or give an image of universality in spiritual visions, ecstasies, and experiences. It sometimes occurs that those who are favored with certain attainments through following an original fall under the influence of the light of their own existence and—unable to comprehend the place and position of the original—can claim superiority over the original. In order to be preserved from such confusion and deceptions, the principles established by the Legislator of the Shari'a should be taken into consideration.

On account of their being the beginning of everything in the name of all material and spiritual worlds of existence and inherent in the Divine Essence, God Almighty's Attributes have the same qualities as the Divine Essence, in that they do not have any peers, equals, or anything similar to them. However, the All-Majestic, All-High, All-Glorified Being is beyond all Names, Attributes, and Qualities. He is infinitely beyond manifestation, appearance, and emergence, and beyond all vision, unveiling, reasoning, conception, and imagination.

Those who belong to the school of Ibnu'l-'Arabi have seen God Almighty's Names and Attributes as being identical to the Divine Being Himself and regarded this approach as the requirement of God's being the One and the belief in His Oneness. Furthermore, they have regarded the Attributes as being identical to each other. For example, in addition to viewing the Attributes of Power and Knowledge as being identical to the Divine Essence, they have asserted that these two Attributes do not differ from each other. According to them, the Divine Essential Qualities or Characteristics, Attributes, and Names have been manifested in a single composition. They have designated this as the first identification or the rank of Divine Uniqueness, in Which all the Essential Characteristics, Attributes, and Names are summed up, while the manifestation of everything in existence has been designated separately as the second identification and the rank of Divine Unity, in Which the Attributes and Names are considered together with the Divine Essence. As a result of this approach, they have seen the truth or original of contingencies as archetypes, which means that this physical realm does not have an external existence and all the things we observe are no different from images reflected in mirrors, and that, in the words of Mulla Jami', whatever we observe is a figment of the imagination. According to them, the (visible) realm of multiplicity is the collection of these imaginary scenes. This realm has three steps of existence, the first of which is "identification as spirits," the second "identification as ideal forms or immaterial representations," and the third "identification as bodies."

The Sunni Sufis who deal with the subject of the Divine Essence and Attributes, and that of existence according to the essential principles of the Religion, stress the existence of certain Attributes of Glory in addition to the Divine Essence, even though the difference between them is only in the mind. They see the Attributes of Glory as if they are luminous veils of the Divine Essence. In the view of these Sufis, all existent things and beings are mirrors of the Divine Names and act as arenas for the manifestation of the Attributes. All of existence is a bright mirror, an arena for the manifestation of the Existence of the All-Sacred Being; every rank of life of the Life of the All-Living, the Giver of Life; all knowledge of the Knowledge of the All-Knowing; all power and strength of the Power of the All-Powerful, the All-Able; and all speeches are mirrors, arenas for the manifestation of the Speech of the Eternal All-Speaking. All instances of seeing and hearing on all kinds of wavelengths are arenas of the manifestation of the Sight and Hearing of the All-Seeing and the All-Hearing respectively. Considering the difference between the Divine Essence and Attributes—even though the difference is in our minds—they say that the whole universe and whatever is in it act as mirrors and screens for the manifestations of Divine Names and Attributes, not of the All-Sacred Divine Essence. All existent things and beings are shadows or rays of the Attribute of Existence, Which is living; all information or knowledge that human beings have is a reflection of and radiation from the Attribute of Knowledge; all strength and power observed in all existent beings, animate or inanimate, is a reflection of the Attribute of Power. Other Divine Attributes can be considered from this perspective in connection with their functions or acts.

It should however be remembered that Divine Attributes are inseparable from and inherent in the Divine Being, while the attributes that contingent beings have are only shadows or reflections. As stated before, the source or original is something different, while a shadow is yet again a different thing, and whatever is other than the original is still another different thing. For this reason, Muslim theologians tend to describe the attributes that contingencies have as "accidental," for they owe their existence and subsistence to the Divine Attributes. Even though matters of "substance" and "accident" are subjects discussed with respect to the physical realm, the Sufis have not deemed it harmful to use these terms in their approaches to the relationship between the Divine Being and contingencies. Moreover, some of them have gone one step further and maintained that all substances and accidents and all attributes and characteristics subsist by God's being the Self-Subsistent by Whom all subsist. However, there have been some who have gone so far as to claim that whatever exists or the existence as a whole consists in Him or "everything is He;" it is impossible to accept such assertions.

According to the scholars of the essentials of the Religion, Divine Attributes are as if additional to the Divine Essence, without ever implying compositeness for God. This approach is also shared by Sunni Sufis. The existence is never He; whatever there is—substance or accident, attribute or characteristic—is from Him and subsists by His being the Self-Subsistent by Whom all subsist. That everything is from Him and subsists by Him can never mean that there is a continuance or contiguity between the Divine Being and the contingent existence or that the latter is a place for the existence of the Former. The Sufis have maintained that the whole of contingent existence with whatever things, characteristics, and states there are in it consists in the shadows of Divine manifestations. All acts are the shadows of Divine Attributes, and the Attributes are the manifestations of Divine Essential Characteristics. For this reason, everything in the universe is nearer to Him than it is to itself by His absolute nearness to it and their being the shadows of His Attributes.

All things in the universe, animate or inanimate, have their existence, characteristics, and features from the manifestations of the Divine Attributes, such as Life, Knowledge, Hearing, and Sight, etc. Divine Attributes and All-Beautiful Names are living and luminous veils of the All-Sacred Divine Essence, and indicate His Essential Perfection. In fact, He does not need these Attributes; the Attributes are inherent in His Essence. He exists by Himself or His All-Sacred Essence, and is living by Himself or by His All-Sacred

Essence. Other Attributes can be considered from this perspective. That is, He is All-Knowing by Himself or by His Essence; He is All-Speaking by Himself or by His Essence, All-Willing by Himself or His Essence, and so on. As this is true for both His Essential and Positive or Affirmative Attributes (the Attributes which describe Who God essentially is), it is also true for the Attributes connected with the Attribute of Making things Exist, Which is among the Positive or Affirmative Attributes.

Thus, Divine Attributes can also be considered as the veils or screens of His Perfection, the veils of His hidden Lights, and the points of His gracious, self-condescending relationship with things and events. As Divine Dignity and Grandeur use apparent physical causes as veils before God's Acts in the creation and operation of the universe, they have also made Divine Attributes veils before the Divine Essence beyond any modality of quality. The imperceptible and incomprehensible relationship of the Divine Being with things and events requires using veils before the Divine Essence and Acts. Similarly, the use of such veils is also required by the Divine Wisdom before the rays of the Divine Facial Lights. Nevertheless, even though the Divine Attributes have the position of serving as a veil before the Divine Essence, the manifestation of Divine Perfection occurs through these same Attributes. For this reason, this veil may also be considered to be a screen that reflects God in His Uniqueness as the Divine Essence.

In short, Divine Attributes are neither the Divine Essence nor the Divine Being Himself, nor are they detached or separate from Him. They are both veils and mirrors for the All-Sacred Divine Essence, and in His relationship with them the Divine Essence is the incomprehensible Original. As His Being cannot be compared to other beings, neither can His Attributes be compared to the attributes of others. He is the Self-Subsistent, while all other beings subsist by His being the Self-Subsistent by whom all subsist. His Attributes are uncontained by time, having neither a beginning nor an end, and they are living as well. They have the dignity of having the sacredness that is unique to the Divine Being. As for the attributes of all created beings, they are lifeless in themselves and relative in respect of their functions and outcomes. They have neither a substantial existence, nor life, nor knowledge. However, as being able to distinguish these realities from one another depends on having an ever-ready, active knowledge originating from God's Presence, not everyone is able to perceive the truth of the matter.

THE DIVINE ATTRIBUTES FROM THE PERSPECTIVE OF THE ESSENTIALS OR BASIC FOUNDATIONS OF THE RELIGION

Now let us discuss the matter from the viewpoint of respected scholars of Islamic theology.

Even though there are some differences in style between the Sufis and the scholars of Islamic theology in approaching the Divine Attributes and in the language they use, both sides have almost the same opinion on the subject. In fact, the Sufis have based their approach to the creeds of Islam on the opinions of the scholars of Islamic theology or the essentials of the Religion, and have tried to interpret their visions and spiritual observations accordingly.

The scholars of Islamic theology have dealt with Divine Attributes of Glory within the categories of the Essential Attributes, the Positive or Affirmative Attributes, the Attributes in the negative— or the Attributes of Exemption or Freedom—the Attributes of Action, and the Attributes to which the Qur'an or the Prophet refer figuratively; these last usually have a figurative meaning, such as God's establishing Himself on the Supreme Divine Throne, Coming, (Having) Hands, Face, Eye(s), and so on.

THE ATTRIBUTES IN THE NEGATIVE OR THE ATTRIBUTES OF EXEMPTION OR FREEDOM

These Attributes are concepts which express that God Almighty is absolutely free or exempt from any need, defect, fault, or shortcoming such as impotence, poverty, neediness, the need to eat or drink, and to beget or be begotten. Ibrahim Haqqi of Erzurum mentions some of them as follows:

> There is no opposite, nor peer, of my Lord in the universe;
> He is the All-Transcendent and exempt from having a form.
> He has no partners, and He is free from begetting and
> being begotten; He is the Unique, having no equals
> these He mentions in *Suratu'l-Ikhlas*.
> He is neither a body nor a substance,
> nor is He an accident nor of matter.
> He does not eat or drink, nor is He contained by time.
> He is absolutely free from change, alteration, or transformation,
> and from colors and having a shape as well—
> These are His Attributes in the negative.
> He is neither in the heavens nor on the earth;
> Neither on the right nor on the left; neither before nor after;
> He is absolutely free from any direction.
> So He is never contained in space.
> He is God, eternally existent, having
> neither a beginning nor an end.
> His Existence is by Himself, not with any other one—
> by God, this is so.
> He existed while the universe did not exist;
> He is the Unique, the One;
> He needs nothing and no one at all,
> but everyone needs Him.
> Nothing bound by time or space happens to Him;
> nothing is incumbent on Him.
> In whatever He does there are instances of wisdom;
> He does nothing in vain.

Scholars mention many other Attributes of Exemption for the Divine Being. However, these cannot even be restricted to those that they have mentioned, for many things unbecoming to the truths of Divinity and Lordship, which we are acquainted with based on the explicit, indisputable statements of the Qur'an and Hadith, have been put forward from the earliest times and are still being put forward and will be put forward in the future. Therefore, believers do and will continue to declare God's absolute exemption or freedom from such imputations.

THE ESSENTIAL ATTRIBUTES

These are the following six Attributes:

(The All-Holy, Self-)Existence, Oneness, Having No Beginning, Eternal Permanence, Being Unlike the Created, and Self-Subsistence.

These are particular to God and cannot be attributed to anyone or anything other than God. Since the opposites of these Attributes are not in question for the Divine Being, they are also considered to be among the Attributes of Exemption.

Wujud ([The All-Holy, Self-]Existence)

Literally meaning being and being existent, *Wujud* ([The All-Holy, Self-]Existence) is an Essential Attribute of God Almighty and denotes that God's existence is by Himself. Even though some scholars of theology and Sufis have asserted that "Existence is identical to the Divine Being Himself," and have therefore attributed to It certain meanings of Divine Unity, verifying scholars have seen Existence as the title of an Eternal Existence and accepted It as the original source of the physical and metaphysical worlds. Just as all existent things and beings are, in one sense, the shadows of the Light of that Essential Existence, so also it is through aspects of their existence such as contingency, being contained in time and space, being created out of non-existence, having certain, unchanging patterns of existence, and purposes for their existence, and through the order, favoring, wisdom, and mercy that they display through their existence or life, that they also act as witnesses and proofs of the Eternal Existence.

God is such a Necessarily Existent Being that in the same way as all the proofs, signs, indications, and witnesses in both our inner worlds and in the outer world demonstrate His existence and Oneness, our sensations, perceptions, and intuition, which we always feel appear in the depths of our spirits, and the points of reliance and seeking help in our consciences also indicate that Permanent Existence both individually and collectively. All consciences that are open to the life lived at the level of the heart and spirit always speak of Him and proclaim His Existence through an inward sensation and intuition that burst forth from the essence of their existence and more loudly than their external sensations and comprehension and more profoundly than their mental perceptions.

Wahdaniyya (Oneness)

Oneness is an Essential Attribute of God in the sense that God Almighty has no peers, equals, rivals, or opposites in either His Essence or His Attributes. Since this Attribute denotes God's being absolutely exempt or free from having any peers or equals, or any resemblance to any other things or beings, It is also considered to be among the Attributes of Exemption.

The Oneness of the Divine Being does not mean that He is one in terms of number; rather He is One in the sense that He has no partners, peers, equals, or opposites in His Essence, Attributes and Acts. As He is One and Unique in His Essence, He is also peerless and unequalled in His Divinity; it is only He Who is the absolutely Worshipped, Besought, Beloved, and Sought One. The Qur'an, which declares, *Say: "He—(He is) God, (Who is) the All-Unique of Absolute Oneness. God—(God is He Who is) the Eternally Besought One (Himself in no need of anything). He begets not, nor is He begotten. And comparable to Him there is none."* (112:1–4), expresses that He is absolutely One and completely independent of anything.

In every place where His Existence is mentioned and stressed in the Qur'an and the Sunna, His Oneness is also mentioned; where His Oneness is noted, His being the Necessarily Existent One is also emphasized. Let us examine the topic briefly from Bediüzzaman, who dedicated his life to describing and teaching about God's Existence and Oneness:

O friend, everything bears a stamp and seal particular to the One, the Eternally Besought, and has signs testifying that He is its Maker and Owner. If out of the innumerable stamps of His Oneness and seals of His being the Eternally Besought you can look at the "stamp" put on the sheet of the earth in spring, you will see that the following facts indicate and bear witness to Him as brightly as the sun.

On the sheet of the earth, we observe acts of ever-original, wise, and purposeful creation. Now notice the following facts and see that wise and purposeful creation:

The act of creation on the earth occurs in infinite abundance.

Together with infinite abundance, it occurs with absolute ease, through an absolute power and with perfect artistry.

Everything is created at an incredible speed but in perfect order and arrangement.

Things are created in absolute abundance and with the greatest economy or at the lowest cost imaginable, yet every individual is unique and priceless.

Despite innumerable causes of disorder and confusion, everything is brought into existence with extraordinary distinction.

Despite the vast distances in time and space and world-wide distribution, there is the highest correspondence and similarity between and among individuals and species.

Despite the highest correspondence and similarity, and though generated from similar or even the same materials, structural principles, and organization, they are in perfect balance and order with an absolute variety and a perfect individualization of characters and features.

The wise and purposeful creation, perfect ease and artistry despite the absolute abundance; the perfect order, arrangement, proportion, and firmness despite the incredible speed; the uniqueness and highest value of every individual despite the absolute abundance and the greatest economy; the extraordinary distinction despite the innumerable causes of disorder and confusion; the highest correspondence and similarity despite the world-wide distribution; the perfect individualization of characters and features and distinction despite the highest correspondence and similarity and being generated from similar or even the same materials, structural principles, and organization are such witnesses for both the Existence and Oneness of the Necessarily Existent One that it would be absolute blindness and obstinacy not to recognize these witnesses, each of which has the strength of thousands of proofs.[62]

Qidam (Having No Beginning)

God Almighty exists free of time; He has no beginning and His existence does not rest on a cause previous to Him. His Attribute of Having No Beginning is a blessed title of His being eternal in the past in connection with His Name the First, and is the basis of the celebrated Name *al-Muqaddim* (the One Who causes to advance).

All Muslim scholars, to whichever school of thought they belong, are in agreement that Having No Beginning is one of the Essential Attributes of the Divine Being. Interpreting this in the meaning of God Almighty being absolutely free from and independent of any causes previous to Him, they have used the following statement concerning this Attribute of the All-Sacred One: "He is the First, Eternal in the past, without having a beginning."

Both the Attribute of *Qidam* (Having No Beginning) and the celebrated Name *al-Qadim* (One with no beginning) mark the Divinity of God Almighty. They denote that God's existence has no beginning and that non-existence is not applicable to the All-Holy Existence. The opposite of Having No Beginning is being existent in time, from which God, exalted is His Majesty, is absolutely free.

Baqa (Eternal Permanence)

Eternal Permanence is one of God's Essential Attributes and is related to the Name the Last, similar to the relationship of the Attribute of Having No Beginning and the Name the First. The Qur'an and the Sunna indicate this Attribute sometimes explicitly and sometimes allusively, and refer to God's eternal permanence either through the Name the Last singly or the Names the First and the

---

62 *al-Mathnawi al-Nuri – Seedbed of the Light* (trans.), New Jersey, 2007, pp., 49–50.

Last together. In addition to frequently reminding us that everything is perishable except Him, the Qur'an makes references to His
Eternal Permanence by mentioning Him with His Names the First
and the Last. Our Prophet, upon him be peace and blessings, also
reminds us of God's Attributes of Having No Beginning and Eternal Permanence in some of his sayings or prayers, such as: "O
God! You are the First; there is nothing before You. You are the
Last; there is nothing after You."[63] The Attributes of Having No
Beginning and Eternal Permanence have approximate meanings
and implications. It is this relationship or approximation which has
led scholars to establish the undeniable, logical argument: "The
non-existence of one who exists eternally is inconceivable." In addition, it is also important that in demonstrating the relationship
between these two Attributes verifying scholars usually mention
them together.

Scholars have expressed the Attribute of Eternal Permanence
sometimes with the phrase "the Undecaying," sometimes with the
phrase "the Undying," and sometimes with the phrase "the Imper-
ishable." All of these words have almost the same meaning.

In addition to the scholars who have seen the Attribute of Eternal Permanence as one of the Essential Attributes like (the All-Holy Self-)Existence, there have been some who have regarded It as
being among the Positive or Affirmative Attributes or the Attributes
Which describe Who God is, such as Life, Knowledge, and Power;
they say: "God is eternally permanent with a permanence that is
particular to His Essence." There have also been some who have
considered It to be among the Attributes of Exemption and have
used Eternal Permanence in the meaning of God being absolutely
exempt or free from cessation or becoming non-existent.

Another point to mention concerning Divine Eternal Permanence is that creatures will be favored with eternity in the eternal
realm. God is Eternally Permanent, so some creatures will be fa-

---

63 *Muslim*, "Dhikr" 61; *at-Tirmidhi*, "Da'awat" 19, 67.

vored with eternity in the other, eternal realm. However, God's Eternal Permanence is by Himself and inseparable from Him, while the eternality of others is a relative permanence that is absolutely dependent on God's Permanence. The eternality of Paradise and Hell is also due to God's Eternal Permanence, like the eternality with which creatures such as humans, jinn, spirit beings, and angels will be favored.

Muhalafatun lil-hawadith
(Being Unlike the Created)

This Attribute denotes that the All-Majestic, All-High God does not resemble, in any way, any of His creatures in His Essence or Attributes. On account of the fact that the opposites of the Essential Attributes of God Almighty are inconceivable for the Divine Being, this Attribute has also been mentioned among the Attributes of Exemption. The decisive, explicit statements of the Qur'an and the Sunna which state that God has no peers, equals, partners, or opposites point to the truth of His Being Unlike the Created.

While some misguided sects have deviated into likening God to His creatures in some respects, some other schools of creed and thought, such as the *Mu'tazila*[64] and *Jahmiyya*,[65] have gone to the extreme of not recognizing His Attributes to emphasize His being unlike the created. However, the scholars of the *Ahlu's-Sunna* or the Sunni scholars have followed the middle way and, by recognizing God's Attributes and drawing attention to an important, basic difference between the Creator and the creation which is marked by

---

[64] The *Mu'tazilites* or *al-Mu'tazilah:* The school of the Muslim "rationalists" which accorded creative effect to human will and agency, concluding that it is human beings who create their actions. In addition, it denies God Almighty Attributes, claims that God is absolutely obliged to reward those who believe and do good deeds, and punish those who disbelieve. (Tr.)

[65] *Jahmiyya*, founded by Jahm ibn Safwan, who lived in the second century of *Hijra*, is the deviant school of creed whose members deny God Attributes and humanity free will, attribute space to God, and claim that the Qur'an is created. (Tr.)

the Attribute of Being Unlike the Created, emphasize that God is unlike the created in both His Essence and Attributes. They conclude: "Whatever comes to your mind concerning the Divine All-Transcending Being, He is beyond it."

Qiyam bi-nafsihi (Self-Subsistence)

God's Being Self-Subsistent means He subsists by Himself in absolute independence of anything else and without needing anything, either in His existence or subsistence, while everything and everyone other than Him owes both their existence and subsistence to Him. On account of any meaning opposite to this Attribute being inconceivable for the Divine Being, this Attribute is also regarded as being among the Attributes of Exemption. Although this Attribute of Glory is not explicitly mentioned in the Qur'an, all the verses concerning God's self-subsistence and maintaining the whole of creation also point to His Self-Subsistence.

Muslim theologians have explicitly stressed God's absolute independence of and freedom from time and space, and from everything else, whether it be a substance or an accident, material or immaterial. They have regarded the physical causes and means that He employs in His Acts and executions as the veils of His Dignity and Grandeur. In the words of Bediüzzaman, Divine Dignity and Grandeur require that physical causes must be veils before the Hand of Power in the sight of the intellect, so that the Power's relationship with some unpleasant and insignificant-seeming things and affairs will not be seen.

THE POSITIVE OR AFFIRMATIVE ATTRIBUTES

The Attributes Whose existence is indispensable and mark God's absolute Perfection have been called the Positive or Affirmative Attributes. God has Life, has perfect Knowledge of everything and an overwhelming Power over everything. He has also a Will Which determines whatever It wishes, however it wishes. In short, these

Attributes make God known to us and describe Who He is through affirmative expressions. Like the Essential Attributes, the opposites of these Attributes cannot be conceived for the All-Holy Being, and all of these Attributes are eternal both in the past and in the future, for they are among the sacred Attributes that are inherent in or inseparable from the All-Majestic, All-High Being with absolute perfection.

As discussed in books on Islamic creed, some of these Attributes such as Life, Knowledge, Power, and Will are in the infinitive form (in the Arabic), while others are in an adjectival form. Humans, jinn, spirit beings, and angels also have these attributes, but when ascribed to the Divine Being, they are absolute, timeless (eternal in the past and in the future), and inherent in Him. Other beings have them as reflections of the same Attributes of God, and these attributes are restricted.

With the exception of the Attribute of Making Exist or Creation, for which there are different considerations, all of the Positive or Affirmative Attributes are veils before the Dignity and Grandeur of the Divine Being, Who has no beginning, is eternally permanent, and infinitely encompassing. They are Attributes of Majesty and Grace that are inherent in the All-Sacred Being, Which subsist by Him, but are not nominally identical to the Divine Being Himself. They are Life, Knowledge, Hearing, Sight, Will, Power, Speech, and Making Exist.

Hayah (Life)

Life is one of the eternal Divine Attributes of Glory, and—provided we do not ignore that Life is an Attribute of the Being that It describes—the sole source of life for all the worlds of living beings. It is solely God Who gives life to and maintains everything in the heavens and on the earth, on land and in water, and in both the physical and metaphysical realms. Every existent thing and being in this world is favored with life by Him and will also be favored with a second life in the other world by Him.

Through the perpetual Divine Attribute of Life, every living being experiences its near and distant environment, builds relationships with these environments, and becomes as if a universal being
while it is a particular. God bestows on everything a great profundity and every being gains a different expansion through this connection. While the Attribute of Life, Which is a veil for the All-Independent Being described by It, shows Itself with Its manifestations and
reflections in all the worlds of living beings, It is never subjected to
division or separation from the All-Sacred One Whom It describes.
It is absolutely free from all such instances of exposure.

The Attribute of Life has priority to other Affirmative Attributes, for Attributes like Power, Will, and Knowledge cannot be
without Life; it is not possible to think about these without considering Life. The manifest Qur'an draws the attention to that perpetual Life in many of its verses and reminds us of the reality, "He is
All-Living, and never dies." The spirit is a general manifestation of
Life, and the state of being alive is Its reflection. In His Speech (the
Qur'an), God calls attention to the celebrated Names the All-Living and the Giver of life as the background of life and He emphasizes that perpetual Life in different manners in connection with
Prophets Adam and Jesus, and with all other living beings. The Ultimate Truth should be viewed through the telescope of life. Everyone who looks through belief can read on the face of life such truths
as: "It is He Who causes to die, Who revives, and Who will restore
everything to a new life in the other realm; it is also He Who will
return the bones, rotten and mixed with earth, to life in a different fashion with their essential parts."

'Ilm (Knowledge)

On account of being related to everything the existence of which is
either necessary, contingent or inconceivable, Knowledge is the Attribute Whose area of comprehension is the broadest; it is also the
origin of contingencies. Reminding us of this breadth, the manifest
Qur'an declares:

With Him are the keys to the Unseen; none knows them but He. And He knows whatever is on land and in the sea; and not a leaf falls but He knows it; and neither is there a grain in the dark layers of earth, nor anything green or dry, but is (recorded) in a Manifest Book (6:59)

Do you not consider that God knows whatever is in the heavens and whatever is on the earth? There is not a secret counsel between three persons but He is the fourth among them, nor between five but He is the sixth among them, nor less than that, nor more, but He is with them wherever they may be. Thereafter, He will make them truly understand all that they do (and call them to account) on the Day of Resurrection. Surely God has full knowledge of everything (58:7).

By reminding us of the infinite area of comprehension of Divine Knowledge, the Qur'an both stirs up our feelings of appreciation and admiration and calls us to self-possession and alertness.

Like other Attributes of Glory, the Divine Attribute of Knowledge never resembles the knowledge of angels, humans, jinn, or spirit beings. God's Knowledge encompasses everything and nothing is outside this limitless, all-encompassing circle. This Knowledge has also nothing to do with increase or decrease, development or perfection, or acquisition. Just as the Ultimate Truth knows Himself through this Knowledge that is inherent in Him, He also knows whatever has happened, whatever will happen, and whatever is impossible to happen. However, God's knowledge of what we call "contingent things or beings"—those whose external existence is not necessary, but possible—does not necessitate their existence. They owe their external existence to the Divine Will's preference that they come into external existence to their remaining only in Knowledge; as a result of this preference the Divine Power brings them into existence.

Another point that indicates the broadness of the sphere which Divine Knowledge encompasses is the beauty, order, arrangement, harmony, wisdom, and observance of the maximum use and benefits that we observe throughout the universe. These are the outcomes of the determination of Knowledge and the truth-speaking witnesses of the All-Knowing, the All-Wise One. They originate from Him and proclaim Him most loudly.

God's Knowledge relates to both eternity in the past and eternity in the future. However, His Knowledge being pre-eternal does not require the pre-eternity of the contents of this Knowledge. Knowledge is something, identification is something different, and the intermediary and ideal existence is different again, and the physical existence is completely different. God Almighty has absolute knowledge and dominion of everything, large or small, particular or universal, material or immaterial, with their types of existence in all these stages or dimensions.

Sam'a (Hearing)

Through His transcendent Attribute of Hearing, God Almighty listens to and hears all sounds and voices, whether they be hidden or in the open, inward or articulate, whispered or expressed out loud, and answers those that He wills to answer. In relation to God, there is no difference at all between inward sighs and lamentations or resounding wailings and cries. Also, His hearing millions of sounds or voices at the same instant does not prevent Him from hearing and answering millions of others. With whatever mouths billions of beings speak, He hears and answers all of them without the least confusion.

On numerous occasions, the Qur'an and the Sunna emphasize that God is the All-Hearing and the All-Seeing, but no explanations are offered concerning the nature of His hearing and seeing; rather the matter is referred to God Almighty, as are the other Attributes. Just as the true nature of the All-Holy Creator is beyond perception, so too are His Knowledge, Hearing, and Seeing or Sight imperceptible, and they will remain so. We see with our eyes, hear with our ears, and speak with our mouth, whereas God does not need any such organs to see, hear, or speak. He is absolutely free and exempt from anything implying personification or comparison.

Basar (Sight)

Sight is one of God's Positive, or Affirmative, Attributes. Through this Attribute of Glory, God Almighty sees everything, large or small, mighty or insignificant, material or spiritual, earthly or heavenly, and protects and cares for whatever and whoever He wills, with nothing remaining hidden from Him. With the same clarity, He sees into the depths of the darkness and the illuminated heavens, He discerns the deepest, darkest corners of the strata of the earth, observes the microscopic, atomic and sub-atomic objects and beings, perceives the most hidden living beings and their most secreted parts, and has knowledge of everything, be it hidden or in the open.

The Attribute of Sight is not mentioned in the Qur'an in Its own, infinitive form, but is referred to with the Divine Name the All-Seeing. This Name is sometimes mentioned singly and sometimes together with the Name the All-Hearing. As with the other Divine Attributes, where this Attribute is mentioned It is mentioned in the affirmative and a warning is made against both the personification of God on one hand and the denial of the Attribute on the other.

The functions of seeing and hearing in human beings have been made dependent on many physical means, causes, and conditions, whereas the Divine Being needs neither physiological nor psychological means or causes, nor any other thing of a similar nature. He sees by Himself through the veil of certain Attributes, He also hears by Himself, and knows by Himself. Even though He sees, hears, and knows by Himself, His Knowledge, Hearing, and Sight are all different from one another. It is manifest misguidance to ascribe all these acts only to the Attribute of Knowledge and to ignore other sacred Attributes. The expressions of some Sufis implying this misguidance are due to certain spiritual states like absorption and spiritual intoxication, and are based on the doctrine of the Unity of Being. The final, decisive judgment in every matter always rests with the Qur'an, according to which God is the All-

Knowing through (the veil of) His Knowledge, the All-Hearing through (the veil of) His Hearing, and the All-Seeing through (the veil of) His Sight.

Irada (Will)

Will is an Affirmative Attribute of God that is inherent in Him; Will determines what will be created and when, where, and how. Whatever God wills to be, whenever, wherever, and however He wills it to be, it is thus. He has certain instances of wisdom in or wise purposes for whatever He does and creates, but these instances of wisdom and purposes do not cause or compel Him to create or do anything. Ibrahim Haqqi of Erzurum says:

> No one can ever compel Him to do something;
> Whatever He Himself wills to create, it comes into existence.

Mashia is another word which is sometimes used in place of *Irada*. Our master, upon him be the most perfect blessings and peace, used this word in different forms in his morning and evening prayers, saying: "Whatever God wills is, whatever God does not will, is not."[66]

It is apparently the Attribute of Will Which determines whether something will or will not be and if it will be, then when, where, and how it will be. The manifest Qur'an emphasizes God's Attribute of Will in many of its verses, such as the following ones, and reminds us of Will's encompassing area of manifestation:

> *To God belongs the sovereignty of the heavens and the earth. He creates whatever He wills. He grants to whom He wills daughters, and grants to whom He wills sons* (42:49).

> *When God wills evil for a people, it cannot be averted, and apart from Him, they have no protector* (13:11).

---

[66] *Abu Dawud,* "Sunna" 6, "Adab" 101.

Say: "Who is there that can hinder God from it, if He wills evil for you, or if He wills mercy for you?" They will not find for themselves, apart from God, either guardian or helper (33:17).

When He wills a thing to be, He but says to it "Be!" and (in the selfsame instant,) it is (36:82).

Say (to them): "Who is there that can intervene on your behalf with God if He wills harm for you or if He wills a benefit for you?" (48:11)

Say: "O God, absolute Master of all dominion! You give dominion to whom You will, and take away dominion from whom You will, and You exalt and honor whom You will, and abase whom You will; in Your hand is all good; surely You have full power over every-thing." (3:26)

God's Will concerns both the creation and operation of the universe and the worldly life of creatures, and the religious life of conscious beings. His Will concerning the creation, operation, and worldly life of creatures is the determining Attribute in the creation and life of creatures at a certain time and place and with certain qualities. As mentioned before, when God Almighty says to something "Be!" at a certain time and place and in the way He wills, it immediately is; while whatever He does not will to be remains in non-existence until He wills it to be. The expression, "'Be!' and it is," which is mentioned many times in the Qur'an, acts as the cipher for a very important truth.

The Divine commands of the creation and operation of the universe that issue from the Divine Will are obeyed absolutely, but obedience to the Divine religious commands has been left to human free will. God orders belief, an Islamic life, and excellence in worship and conduct, showing humans the way to being true humans. If humans display an inclination by following this way, God gives external existence to this inclination in accordance with His Wisdom and enables His servants to attain true humanity. However, He is never obliged to do anything or give existence to any inclination of His servants in the physical world.

Due to the different benefits and purposes that are beyond human perception, the Divine Will that is related to the operation and life of the universe sometimes wills apparent evils alongside good, and harmful things alongside what is useful; however, His Will relating to religious commands and affairs always wills what is good, beautiful, and useful. However, the responsibility for the apparent evils in the Divine Will's choice concerning human actions and the life of the universe belongs to those who cause them. Human free will, whether it be in the form of an inclination or putting that inclination into action, is a shadow of the Divine Will and is a potential ability to make choices with which humans have been equipped. According to the *Maturidis*, what is called "the universal will" is this potential ability or capacity, while what they call "the particular will" is the inclination and determination to do or not do a particular thing. As for the *Ash'aris*,[67] they prefer calling God's Will "the Universal Will," and the inclination of human beings "the particular will."

Qudra (Power)

Qudra is another Affirmative Attribute of God; *Qudra* means that God is absolutely able to do anything He wills and that He has absolute power over everything. Incapacity, impotence, or powerlessness, all of which are the opposites to Power, cannot be conceived of in connection with the Divine Being. There is nothing over which He does not have absolute power. Everything, from the bottom of the earth to the highest heavens, has been and is being created through that all-overwhelming Power, and it is again through that Power that everything changes forms and states, develops, and is perfected, thus undergoing ceaseless experiences. In

---

67 The *Maturidis*, the followers of Imam Muhammad ibn Muhammad Abu Mansur al-Maturidi (d. 944), and *Ash'aris*, the followers of Imam Abu'l-Hasan al-Ash'ari (d. 665), comprise the *Ahlu's-Sunna wa'l-Jama'a*, the overwhelming majority of Muslims. There are slight differences of opinion between these two branches of the *Ahlu's-Sunna*. (Tr.)

many verses such as the following ones, the Qur'an reminds us of His infinite Power and calls us to turn to that All-Strong, All-Forceful, All-Powerful, All-Omnipotent One:

> *And God's is the sovereignty (absolute ownership and dominion) of the heavens and the earth, and God has full power over everything* (3:189).

> *The matter of the Hour (of Doom) is but the twinkling of an eye, or even quicker. Surely God has full power over everything* (16:77).

> *And so, God is He Who is the Absolute Truth and Ever-Constant, and He gives life to the dead, and He has full power over everything* (22:6).

> *Say: "Go about on the earth and see how God originated creation. Then God will bring forth the other (second) creation (in the form of the Hereafter). Surely God has full power over everything* (29:20).

> *Blessed and Supreme is He in Whose Hand is the Sovereignty; and He has full power over everything* (67:1).

> *By no means is God One Whom anything whatever in the heavens or on earth can frustrate (in His decrees). Surely He is All-Knowing, All-Powerful* (35:44).

Despite insignificant differences of view concerning the relation of the Divine Power with things and events, all scholars of the *Ahlu's-Sunna* are in agreement that Power is among the eternal, Affirmative Attributes of God Almighty.

Kalam (Speech)

Speech is another of God's Affirmative Attributes, Which marks His Perfection. All religious commands and all decrees and directions that come on different wavelengths in the form of Revelation and inspiration, with their unique nature, have originated from that Attribute. In many verses like the following, the Qur'an not only presents the Attribute of Speech explicitly or implicitly, but also reminds us of the fact that all Divine Words that issued from His Attribute of Speech and Which were manifested in the form of Revelation were of the same basic nature for all Prophets:

Of those Messengers, some We have exalted above others (in some respects). Among them are those to whom God spoke (in a peculiar fashion), and He raised some others in degrees (2:253).

> It is not for any mortal that God should speak to him unless it be by Revelation or from behind a veil, or by sending a messenger (angel) to reveal, by His leave, whatever He wills (to reveal). Surely He is All-Exalted, All-Wise (42:51).

> And Messengers We have already told you of before, and Messengers We have not told you of; and God addressed Moses and spoke to Him (4:164).

> And He revealed to His servant what He revealed (53:10).

> We have revealed to you (O Messenger), as We revealed to Noah and the Prophets after him; and We revealed to Abraham, Ishmael, Isaac, Jacob and the Prophets who were raised in the tribes among his progeny, and Jesus, Job, Jonah, Aaron, and Solomon; and We gave David the Psalms (4:163).

> And just so We reveal to you a Qur'an (a Recitation) in Arabic so that you may warn the mother-city and all those around it (42:7).

The noble Qur'an is a manifestation of Divine Speech in keeping with the time from when it began to be revealed to the Day of Resurrection, and with the Prophet to whom it was addressed, and to the community to which it was sent. Divine Speech manifested Itself in the particular form of a Divine Book for each community in which It was revealed. Both the Attribute of Divine Speech, Which is the source of the Divine Books, and the Divine Books in their essence are eternal in the past. So, on account of their essence, which is described as "God's speech to or in Himself," none of the Divine Books are created. However, their written forms as books or their recitations are created. Their written forms and recitations are described as "the Speech in words."

If there is a Divine Book Which originated from the Divine Attribute of Speech and has remained intact in its original form, it is the noble Qur'an. From the very first day when it began to be revealed, it has remained without undergoing the least change, thanks to God's protection and the sincere efforts of its faithful followers. The richness of its contents, the conservation of its freshness as if it was being revealed anew in every age, and its power and profundity in solving all spiritual, emotional, mental, economic, social, administrational, and political problems, are another guarantee for its indispensability. It is for this reason that what is meant and reminded of by the phrase "the Divine Word" has been the noble Qur'an.

Takwin (Making Exist)

Takwin, which means making or causing to exist, according to the *Maturidi*s, is the eighth of the Affirmative Attributes of God Almighty.

God is the Creator of everything, and the Attribute of Making Exist is the Attribute of Glory that is the origin of this creation. The All-Exalted Creator, Who introduces Himself as the Creator of the heavens and the earth, prepares everything He creates for existence through His all-encompassing Knowledge, His all-embracing Will, Which determines what will be sent into the arena of existence and when, where, and with what characteristics, and His all-overwhelming Power, Which is all-able to do whatever His Will determines; and He finally refers this to the veil of His Attribute of Making Exist. The whole universe with whatever is in it, everything animate or inanimate, all with different designs, styles, and natures, comes into existence through His creation, invention, and origination. The sacred Attributes are veils before this Act of God Almighty, and the Attribute of Making Exist is another curtain before the Will and the Power. Everything of contingency is established within a broad frame by the Knowledge; the Will selects between many probabilities, while the Power marks its possibility to be or to come into existence, and the Attribute of Making Exist manufactures it on Its own workbench, presenting what has been created to the View of the Eternal Witness.

Making Exist is, according to the *Maturidis*, among the independent, eternal, and substantial Affirmative Attributes. The *Ash'aris'* approach is slightly different; according to them, this Attribute is of nominal or relative existence. For if something which the Divine Will has judged to exist is brought into existence through the Power and Will, there is no further need for Making Exist. The *Ash'aris* have this same approach for other Attributes of actions that relate to Making Exist. They view them as Attributes that are not eternal in the past, but which emerged later; they explain every occurrence with the Power and Will. However, it is God Who knows best.

THE ATTRIBUTES OF ACTION

As for the Attributes of action, briefly, they are six and are as follows: Creation, Originating Uniquely, Producing, Giving Life and Reviving, Causing to Die, and Providing.

Khalq (Creation)

Literally meaning originating out of nothing and formation, *khalq* (creation) denotes that God originates something when nothing of it exists and makes it with all of its essential elements. With this meaning, creation cannot be attributed to any other than God Almighty.

Khalq is used in the Qur'an also in the meanings of making up, fabricating, and giving form to clay. While it can be used for created beings with these meanings, the Qur'an attributes creation only to God. Likewise, the attributes of *Khaliq* (the Creator) and *Khallaq* (the Supreme Creator), which are derived from *khalq*, are used only in attribution to God.

There is a difference between the sacred Attribute of Creation (*Khalq*) and the majestic Attribute of Making Exist (*Takwin*), as well as between the Attributes of Originating Uniquely (*Ibda'*) and Producing (*Insha'*), which are regarded to have originated from the latter. This difference is as follows: Creation means giving existence to something with its essential parts and building blocks, Originating Uniquely means creating without having any precursor to imitate and creating in a unique and peerless way, Producing denotes bringing about something by arranging its parts which have already been created, while Making Exist, Which encompasses almost all of these meanings, signifies bringing into existence by giving Its own hue to all the Attributes of action.

It is God alone Who creates everything particular or universal, small or large, earthly or heavenly, animate or inanimate, spiritual or corporeal, and it is also He Who creates all states and the acts of all beings during their entire life. In many of its illuminating statements, the noble Qur'an reminds us that it is exclusively God Who originates, creates, and produces. For example:

> *It is He Who created all that is on the earth for you (2:29).*

> *All praise and gratitude are for God, Who has created the heavens and the earth, and brought into being veils of darkness and the light (6:1).*

> *Indeed your Lord is God, Who has created the heavens and the earth in six "days" (7:54; 10:3).*

> *Do they never consider that God Who has created the heavens and the earth is able to create them anew (the dead) in their own likeness? (17:99).*

> *And He it is Who from a fluid has created human and made it (a male and female and, through them,) into a population through descent and marriage. And Your Lord is All-Powerful (25:54).*

> *God is He Who creates you, then He sustains you (by providing for you), then He causes you to die, and then He will bring you to life again (30:40).*

> *All-Glorified is He, Who has created the pairs all together out of what the earth produces, as well as out of themselves, and out of what they do not know (36:36).*

It is God Who has created you and all that you do (37:96).

Have they (the unbelievers) not considered that surely God, Who has created the heavens and the earth, and never wearied with their creation, is able to bring the dead to life? Certainly He is; He has full power over everything (46:33).

Ibda' (Originating Uniquely)

Ibda' means that God Almighty creates without there be anything before to imitate and in a unique, unequalled, and unprecedented way. In place of *ibda'*, the words *ihdas* (innovation), *ihtira'* (creating out of nothing), *ijad* (invention), and *sun'* (making) can be used, although there are slight differences among them. In fact, these words express different aspects of *Takwin* (Making Exist). In several verses such as the following ones, the manifest Qur'an presents to our view God's unprecedented origination and calls upon us to notice the beauties of His Art:

The Originator of the heavens and the earth with nothing preceding Him to imitate. When He decrees a thing, He does but say to it, "Be!" and it is (2:117).

The Originator of the heavens and the earth with nothing before Him to imitate (6:101).

Insha' (Producing)

Literally meaning gathering together certain ingredients or components and elements to produce a new thing, *Insha'* is the Attribute of God which denotes gathering together certain essential ingredients or components that have already been created to produce something new. In dozens of explicit verses, the glorious Qur'an reminds us of this mighty reality. For example:

He it is Who produces gardens (and vineyards, and orchards) trellised and untrellised, and date-palms, and crops varying in taste, and olives, and pomegranates, resembling one another and yet so different (6:141).

He it is Who has made for you (the faculty of) hearing, and eyes, and hearts (23:78).

He it is Who developed you from a single human self and has appointed for each of you a lodging-place where you will stay permanently, and a place where you will stay temporarily (6:98).

Say: "He Who produced them in the first instance will give them life (anew)" (36:79).

Ihya' and Imata (Giving Life and Reviving, and Causing to Die)

Both *Ihya'*, which means granting life, favoring with life, and reviving, and *Imata*, which means causing to die or dealing with death, are among the Attributes of action of the Giver of Life and the One Who causes death. These two Attributes are mentioned in the Qur'an in different verb forms, sometimes together and sometimes separately. Some examples are as follows:

Surely in the creation of the heavens and the earth, and the alternation of night and day, and the vessels sailing in the sea with profit to people, and the water that God sends down from the sky, therewith reviving the earth after its death and dispersing therein all kinds of living creatures, and His disposal of the winds, and the clouds subservient between the sky and earth—surely there are signs (demonstrating that He is the One God deserving worship, and the sole Refuge and Helper) for a people who reason and understand (2:164).

God sends down from the sky water and therewith revives the earth after its death. Surely in that there is a sign for people ready to hear (the truth) (16:65).

A clear sign for them (of God's Oneness and Lordship) is the dead earth: We revive it and bring forth from it grain (36:33).

And He it is Who causes to die and gives life (53:44).

How can you disbelieve in God, seeing that you were dead, and He gave you life? Then He causes you to die. Then He will bring you to life again; and then you will be returned to Him (2:28).

They will say: "Our Lord! You have made us die twice, and given us life twice, so we acknowledge our sins" (40:11).

Abraham said, "My Lord is He Who gives life and causes to die." (2:258).

Surely it is also We, We Who give life and cause to die (15:23).

God (He alone) gives life and causes to die; and whatever you do, God sees it well (3:156).

Tarziq (Providing)

Literally meaning providing, sustaining, and maintaining, *tarziq* is also among the Attributes of action. Everything from food and beverages to whatever we need for our physical, mental, and spiritual life is included in the meaning of the word *rizq* (provision) and, therefore, everything is provided by God, the All-Providing. In dozens of verses, such as the following ones, the Qur'an of miraculous exposition reminds us that God is the All-Providing for all of creation and emphasizes His majestic Attribute of Providing:

> *O you who believe! Eat of the pure, wholesome things that We have provided for you, and (in return) give thanks to God, if you worship Him alone* (2:172).

> *Those who believe in the Unseen, establish the Prayer in conformity with its conditions, and out of what We have provided for them they spend (in God's cause and for the needy)* (2:3).

> *We do not ask you to provide for Us; rather, it is We Who provide for you* (20:132).

> *Say: "Who is it that provides for you from heaven and earth…?"* (10:31)

> *Surely those that you worship instead of God do not have power to provide for you; so seek all your provision from God, and worship Him and be thankful to Him* (29:17).

> *God enlarges provision for whom He wills of His servants, and straitens it (for whom He wills). Surely God has full knowledge of everything* (29:62).

In addition to those explained above, it is possible to mention many other Attributes of action related to the Attribute of Making Exist, such as Arrangement, Beautification, Making Happy, Bestowing Bounties, Making Victorious, and Defeating. But since we intended only to give a brief explanation of the Divine Attributes of Glory, let us not go beyond the limit of our intentions and put a halt to our discussion here.

> O God! I ask You for Your forgiveness, health, resignation to all Your decrees and judgments, regard for and attention toward You; I pray for Your relieving breezes, Your intimacy, Your nearness, and Your love. And bestow blessings and peace on the noblest one of Your creatures, our master Muhammad, and on his good and pure Family and Companions.

GOD'S FIGURATIVE ATTRIBUTES

> I later realized that I had forgotten to write about God's Attributes which are used in the Qur'an and Sunna in a figurative sense. Since a reference was made to them at the beginning of the article on God's Attributes of Glory, it is necessary that I provide brief information about them here.

Although the Figurative Attributes are frequently mentioned in the Qur'an and the Sunna, as it is not proper to ascribe them to the Divine Being with their apparent meanings, different interpretations have been made about them and they have caused some to slip away from the straight path. Some people have approached them in their literal meanings and have not been able to prevent themselves from going to extremes, thus putting themselves at the risk of falling into misguidance and loss. However, while the earliest, upright Muslim scholars preferred to keep aloof from making interpretations about them based on their personal views, their righteous followers never abandoned respect or self-possession in their moderate interpretations, going neither towards denial nor deviating into anthropomorphism or similar creeds.

We encounter the Figurative Attributes both in the Qur'an and the Sunna. Among these Attributes we can list:

- "Coming" in *And Your Lord comes* (89:22);
- "Self-Establishment" in *The All-Merciful, Who has established Himself on the Supreme Throne* (20:5), which means God's subjugating the creation to His command, manifesting His Sovereignty, Grandeur, and Power;
- "Avoidance" in *God avoids but completing His light* (9:32);
- "Self" in *He has bound Himself to mercy* (6:12), *And I have attached you to Myself* (20:41), and in the Prophetic saying, "You are as You have praised Yourself;"[68] and the Prophetic quotation from God, "Surely I have made wrongdoing unlawful for Myself."[69]
- "Wrath" in *God has become wrathful with them* (4:93), which means punishment and condemnation;
- "Hand" in verses such as *God's hand is over their hands* (48:10), and *All grace is in God's hand* (57:29), which means power, ownership, control and disposal, and help;
- "Face" in verses such as *Everything is perishable except His Face* (28:88), *But there remains forever the Face of Your Lord* (55:27), and *"We feed you only for the sake of God's Face"* (76:9), which means the Divine Being Himself or God's approval and good pleasure.
- Further, concepts, such as:
- "Saying" in verses like: *When your Lord said to the angels* (2:30);
- "Speaking" in *His Lord spoke to him* (7:143);
- "All-Hearing, All-Seeing" in the Divine declaration, *Surely God is All-Hearing, All-Seeing* (22:75);

---

68 *Muslim*, "Salah" 222; *at-Tirmidhi*, "Da'awat" 75.
69 *Muslim*, "Birr" 55; Ibn Hanbal, *al-Musnad*, 5:160.

- "Companionship" which is understood from *God is with You* (47:35); and

- "Footing" in *They have a sure footing with their Lord* (10:2),

are regarded by some as being among the same Attributes.

It is possible to encounter many similar Attributes in the sayings of the noblest Prophet, upon him be peace and blessings.

- "Asking" in "He asks the angels;"[70]

- "Ordering" and "Prohibiting" in the Prophetic sayings where we see the phrases "He orders"[71] and "He prohibits;"[72]

- "Witnessing" in the sayings where the phrase "He witnesses"[73] is mentioned;

- "Moving Speedily" in the sayings such as "He moves speedily to respond with favor;"[74]

- "Approaching" in such sayings as "He immediately approaches with favor;"[75]

- "Descending" in the sayings such as "He descends to the heaven of the world,"[76] and several other concepts such as:

- "Loving, Becoming Wrathful, the Best Form, Exhilaration, Smiling, Grasping, Contracting, Expanding, Struggling, Feeling Wonder, Showing Care, Heed and Sensitivity, Being with or Companionship" in the Prophetic sayings where we see the phrases, "He loves;[77] He becomes wrathful;[78] He is seen in the Best Form;[79] He exhilarates;[80]

---

70 *al-Bukhari*, "Mawaqitu's-Salah" 16; *Muslim*, "Masajid" 210.

71 *al-Bukhari*, "Tafsiru'l-Qur'an" 22; *Muslim*, "Salatu'l-Musafirin" 274.

72 *al-Bukhari*, "Maghazi" 38; *Muslim*, "Ayman" 1.

73 *at-Tirmidhi*, "Tafsir" 24; Ibn Hanbal, *al-Musnad*, 5:172.

74 *al-Bukhari*, "Tawhid" 15; *Muslim*, "Dhikr" 2.

75 *al-Bukhari*, "Tawhid" 15; *Muslim*, "Dhikr" 2.

76 *al-Bukhari*, "Tahajjud" 14; *Muslim*, "Salatu'l-Musafirin" 168, 172.

77 *al-Bukhari*, "Manaqibu'l-Esrar" 4; *Muslim*, "Iman" 129.

78 *al-Bukhari*, "Manaqibu'l-Asrar" 4; *Muslim*, "Iman" 129.

79 *at-Tirmidhi*, "Tafsir" (38) 2–4; Ibn Hanbal, *al-Musnad*, 1:368.

80 *al-Bukhari*, "Da'awat" 4; *Muslim*, "Tawba" 2.

He smiles;[81] He grasps;[82] He expands;[83] He struggles;[84] He feels wonder;[85] There is none more careful and sensitive than God,"[86] and "I am with him when He mentions Me,"[87] respectively.

The earliest scholars of Islam, who followed the way of the Prophet and his Companions very closely, acted in self-possession and with great care concerning the Figurative Attributes, in the same way they did with the subtle, very meaningful statements of the Qur'an. They admitted them to be among God's Attributes and preferred referring their true meanings to God Almighty. Unlike these scholars of the *Ahlu's-Sunna wa'l-Jama'a*, the followers of certain misguided sects, such as the Anthropomorphists (*Mujassima*) and the Comparers (*Mushabbiha*), asserted that God Almighty had a body and compared Him to the created, respectively; this was partly in order not to deny these Attributes, and thus the Divine Being was conceived as One Who, like humans, has hands, feet, eyes, and ears, and Who descends, ascends, runs, gets near, becomes rejoiced, and smiles, etc. As a result, they fell into mental misguidance. In contrast to such an extreme attitude as this, the *Mu'tazila* and the *Jahmiyya* went to the opposite extreme and, considering that having such Attributes was not appropriate for the Divine Being, denied God any Attribute, rather asserting that there is only the Divine Being Himself with His acts. However, the earliest, righteous Muslim scholars admitted the existence of all the Divine Attributes including the Figurative Ones, and referred the exact knowledge of their true nature to God Almighty. In addition to their considerations of the Divine Essence and Attributes that are free from any comparison and anthropomor-

---

81　*al-Bukhari*, "Adhan" 129; *Muslim*, "Iman" 299.

82　*al-Bukhari*, "Tawhid" 19; *Muslim*, "Sifatu'l-Munafiqin" 23.

83　*Muslim*, "Tawba" 31; Ibn Hanbal, *al-Musnad*, 4:395.

84　at-Tabarani, *al-Mu'jamu'l-Kabir*, 11:19.

85　*at-Tirmidhi*, "Da'awat" 46; *Abu Dawud*, "Jihad" 74.

86　*al-Bukhari*, "Kusuf" 2; *Muslim*, "Kusuf" 1.

87　*al-Bukhari*, "Tawhid" 15; *Muslim*, "Dhikr" 2.

phism, they were able to view and speak of the Divine Being as absolutely exempt from any defects, resemblance, or partnership, and, in the following words of the scholars of religious essentials or basic principles, they ascertained the truth: "God exists and has Attributes, without having any resemblance and bearing no comparison to anything created; He is absolutely free from any defect, resemblance, and comparison, but has Attributes and Names."

Some of the scholars of later generations did not deem it harmful to make certain reasonable interpretations concerning the Attributes based on the essential principles of the Religion in order to preserve minds from adulteration with misguided thoughts and creeds. For example, they interpreted "Descending" as the descent of God's mercy, "Coming" as the coming of His punishment, "Self-Establishment on the Supreme Throne" as His demonstrating His absolute dominion, "Hand" as His bounties, Power, and ownership, "Moving Speedily" and "Getting Near" as God's immediate response with favor and regard, and "Love" as His treating people pleasingly and mercifully.

Unless there is a necessity to respond to objections, following the way of the earliest righteous scholars is safer and is a better-mannered approach. In case of necessity, the way of the righteous scholars of later generations may be adopted.

> O God! I believe in You and in whatever comes from Your Presence. Enable us to follow Your Religion in safety and make us steadfast. Do not let our hearts swerve after You have guided us, and bestow upon us mercy from Your Presence. Surely You are the All-Bestowing. And bestow Your blessings and peace on our master and the intercessor for our sins, Muhammad, and on his good and pure Family and Companions. All praise and gratitude are for God, the Lord of the worlds.

THE ALL-BEAUTIFUL NAMES OF GOD

Since the time of the Last Messenger, upon him be peace and blessings, the All-Beautiful Names of Godxalted is His Majesty, have been a right-guiding source for knowing and recognizing the Divine Being in accordance with His Attributes of Majesty and Grace, and for protecting those who have been able to study and understand them correctly from straying, and for pouring forth true knowledge about the truth of Divinity to those who have been so protected. Everyone who has set off to acquire true knowledge of God has advanced toward deepening in belief in the bright light of the All-Beautiful Names and in their areas of manifestation. In pursuit of true knowledge and love of God Almighty and in pursuit of spiritual pleasures, they have given these Names into the hands of their outer and inner faculties, like so many mysterious keys that will open the doors of knowing Him in accordance with His "true Nature or Identity;" thus they have advanced toward the horizon of "seeing," knowing, and experiencing Him in the light of the truth that radiates through these doors.

Even though from the earliest days of Islam the All-Beautiful Names have always been a pure source for those who want to have recourse to them for knowledge of God, they began to be studied and discussed systematically in later eras. So many books, brief or detailed, in prose or in verse, have been written about the All-Beautiful Names of God that it is not possible to determine them or to mention all of them. My following citations are only a drop in the ocean:

- *Tafsirul-Asma'ul-Husna* ("The Interpretation of the All-Beautiful Names") by Abu Ishaq az-Zajjaj,[88]

- *Al-Minhaj fi Shu'abil-Iman* ("The Highway Concerning the Branches of Faith") by al-Halimi,[89]

- *Al-Asma' wa's-Sifat* ("The Names and the Attributes") by 'Abdu'l-Qahir al-Baghdadi,[90]

- *Al-Maqsadu'l-Athna' fi Sharhi Asma'ullahi'l-Husna* ("The Best Means in Explaining the All-Beautiful Names of God") by Imam al-Ghazzali,[91]

- *Al-Amadu'l-Aqsa'* ("The Farthest Aim") by Abu Bakr ibnu'l-'Arabi,[92]

- *Lawa'mi'ul-Bayyinat* ("Rays of Clarifications") by Fakhru'd-Din ar-Razi,[93]

---

88 Abu Ishaq Ibrahim ibn as-Sirri az-Zajjaj (d., 924) was a famous philologist and interpreter of the Qur'an. Among his works are Ma'aniu'l-Qur'an, Khalqu'l Insan, and Tafsiru Jami'i'l-Mantiq. (Tr.)

89 Abu 'Abdullah Huseyn ibn Hasan al-Halimi (949–1012) was a famous Shafi'i jurisprudent and scholar of Hadith. He was a judge in al-Bukhara.

90 'Abdu'l-Qahir ibn Tahir ibn Muhammad al-Baghdadi (d., 429) was a jurist, scholar of principles of religion and theology, man of letters, grammarian, and mathematician. He settled in Neyshabur in Khurasan. Among his works are *Bulughu'l-Mada min Usuli'l-Huda*, *Fada'ihu'l-Karramiyya*, and *al-Farq Bayna'l-Firaq*.

91 Imam Abu Hamid Muhammad al-Ghazzali (d. 1111): A major theologian, jurist, and sage who was considered a reviver (of Islam's purity and vitality) during his time. Known in Europe as Algazel, he was the architect of Islam's later development. He wrote many books, the most famous being *Ihyau 'Ulumi'd-Din* ("Reviving the Religious Sciences"). (Tr.)

92 Abu Bakr Ibnu'l-Arabi (d., 1148) was a Muslim from Spain. He was a master of al-Maliki jurisprudence. He also contributed to the spread of Ash'ari theology in Spain. His most famous works are *'Aridatu'l-Ahwazi* (a commentary on *Sunanu't-Tirmidhi*, and *Ahkamu'l-Qur'an*. (Tr.)

93 Abu 'Abdullah Muhammad ibn 'Umar ibni'l-Husayn Fakhru'd-Din ar-Razi (1149–1209) was a very famous Muslim theologian, philosopher, and a commentator on the Qur'an. He was born in Ray, now a district of modern Tehran. He died in Herat, in modern Afghanistan. He also wrote on Islamic law, medicine, physics, astrology, literature, and history. His most famous work is *at-Tafsiru'l-Kabir* ("The Great Commentary on the Qur'an") known as *Mafatihu'l-Ghayb* (Keys to the Unseen). (Tr.)

- *Al-Kitabu'l-Athna' fi Sharhi Asma'ullahi'l-Husna* ("The Book of the Means to Explain the All-Beautiful Names of God") by al-Qurtubi,[94]
- *Al-Jami' li-Asma'il-Husna* ("The Compendious Book of the All-Beautiful Names") which Hamid Ahmad Tahir, Ayman Abdu'r-Razzaq, and Yusuf 'Ali compiled from Ibn Qayyim al-Jawziya,[95] al-Qurtubi, Allama as-Sa'di,[96] Ibn Kathir,[97] and al-Bayhaqi,[98]
- *Kashfu'l-Ma'na an Sirri Asma'illahi'l-Husna* ("Unveiling the Mystery of God's All-Beautiful Names") by Muhyi'd-Din ibnu'l-'Arabi,
- *Asma'ullahi'l-Husna* ("The All-Beautiful Names of God") by 'Abdul-Qadir al-Jilani[99] in prose,

---

94 al-Qurtubi, Imam Abu 'Abdullah Muhammad ibn Ahmad Al-Qurtubi (1214–1273) was a famous Sunni Maliki scholar. He lived in al-Andalus (Muslim Spain) and Egypt. He was specialized in *fiqh* and *hadith*. The most famous of his works is his twenty-volume *tafsir, al-Jami' li-Ahkami'l-Qur'an*. (Tr.)

95 Ibn Qayyim al-Jawziya, Muhammad ibn Abi Bakr (d., 1350): A famous, all-round scholar and a disciple of Ibn Taymiya who is also considered to be among the best representatives of his school of thought. (Tr.)

96 Allama 'Abdu'r-Rahman ibn Nasir as-Sa'di (1889–1956) was a prominent scholar. He was born and lived in Saudi Arabia. He wrote on matters concerning Islamic jurisprudence, Hadith, Qur'anic commentary, and language. Among his works are *Taysiru'l-Karim ar-Rahman fi Tasfsiri'l-Qur'an, Minhaju's-Salikin* and *al-Qawa'in wa'l-Usulu'l-Jami'a wa'l-Furuq wa't-Taqasimi'l-Badi'ati'n-Nafi'a*. (Tr.)

97 Abu Al-Fida, 'Imadu'd-Din Isma'il ibn 'Umar ibn Kathir was a famous scholar (1301–1373). He was born in 1301 in Busra, Syria, and studied Islamic jurisprudence, Hadith, Qur'anic commentary, and history. He died in Damascus. Among his famous works are his commentary on the Qur'an known as *Tafsiru Ibn Kathir*, and *al-Bidaya wa'n-Nihaya*. (Tr.)

98 Abu Bakr Ahmad ibn Husayn al-Bayhaqi, known as Imam Al-Bayhaqi (994–1066) was born Khurasan. He was a famous hadith scholar. He also an expert in Islamic jurisprudence. Among his most well-known books are *as-Sunanu'l-Kubra*, commonly known as *Sunanu'l-Bayhaqi, al-Mabsut, Dala'ilu'n-Nubuwwa* and *al-Asma' wa's-Sifat*. (Tr.)

99 'Abdu'l-Qadir al-Jilani (d., 1166): One of the most celebrated Sufi masters. A student of jurisprudence and Hadith, he became known as the "Spiritual Pole" of his age and the "the Greatest Means of Divine Help." Among his well-known books are *Kitabu'l-Ghunya, Futuhu'l-Ghayb*, and *Al-Fathu'r-Rabbani*. (Tr.)

- *Al-Maqsadu'l-Athna' fi Sharhi Asma'ullahi'l-Husna* ("The Best Means in Explaining the All-Beautiful Names of God") by Ahmad ibn Ahmad Zarruq,[100]
- *Sharhu Asma'illahi'l-Husna* ("Explaining the All-Beautiful Names of God"), by Abu'l-Qasim al-Qushayri,[101]
- *Sharhi Asma'i'l-Husna* ("Explaining the All-Beautiful Names") by Muhammed İbrahim Efendi in Turkish,
- *Kur'an'da Uluhiyet* (Divinity in the Qur'an) by Professor Suat Yıldırım,[102]

can be cited with appreciation and prayers to God that they may be favored with the approval of God Almighty.

The All-Beautiful Names are God's Names of Glory Which mean the All-Beautiful and All-Exalted Names. The Divine Names are mentioned with this title both in the Qur'an and the accurately related sayings of our master, the Prophet, upon him be peace and blessings. Among these Names, *Allah* (God) is in the form of noun, while the others are in the form of adjectives. The glorious Name *Allah* (God), Which is the Word of Majesty, is the all-glorious Title of the Divine Essence, Which encompasses all the other Names; it is not possible to expresses Its meaning with another word.

---

[100] Ahmad ibn Ahmad Zarruq (1442–1493) was a Muslim scholar and Shadhili Sufi from Morocco. He traveled and studied is Morocco, Algeria, Tunis, Cairo and Hejaz. He studied Qur'anic commentary, Hadith, Islamic jurisprudence, and language. Among his famous works are *Qawa'idu't-Tasawwuf*, *I'tina'u'l-Fawaid*, and *Sharhu'l-Haqa'iq wa'd-Daqa'iq*. (Tr.)

[101] Abdu'l-Karim ibn Hawazin al-Qushayri (986–1074) was a Muslim Sufi scholar and master. He also studied Islamic jurisprudence, Qur'anic commentary, Hadtih, and theology. His major works are *ar-Risala* ("The Treatise on Sufism") and *Lata'ifu'l-Isharat*. His *Risala* has had great influence on Sunni Sufism and Sufis. (Tr.)

[102] Suat Yıldırım (1941–) is a contemporary Turkish scholar. He was born in Diyarbakır, a province in south-east Turkey, and studied in Theology School affiliated with Ankara University. He worked as a mufti and then specialized in Qur'anic commentary. He taught in different theology schools. Among his well-known works are *Kur'an'da Uluhiyet* ("Divinity in the Qur'an") and *Peygamberimizin Kur'an'ı Tefsiri* ("Prophetic Interpretation of the Qur'an"). (Tr.)

Among the All-Beautiful Names, those such as *al-Quddus* (The All-Holy and All-Pure), *as-Salam* (The Supreme Author of peace and salvation), *al-Ahad* (The Unique One of absolute Oneness), and *al-Wahid* (The One of absolute Unity) mark, like the Attributes of Exemption, the all-holiness, all-purity, and absolute uniqueness of the Divine Being. The all-glorious Names *al-Hayy* (the All-Living), *al-'Alim* (the All-Knowing), *as-Sami'* (the All-Hearing), *al-Basir* (the All-Seeing), *al-Murid* (the All-Willing), *al-Qadir* (the All-Powerful), and *al-Mutakallim* (the All-Speaking) appear as translators of the Positive or Affirmative Attributes; the all-sacred Names, such as *al-Khaliq* (the Creator), *al-Mubdi* (the All-Initiating), *al-Muhyi* (the All-Reviving, the Giver of Life), *al-Mumit* (The One Who causes to die), *ar-Razzaq* (the All-Providing), *al-Wahhab* (the All-Bestowing), *al-Ghaffar* (the All-Forgiving), *as-Sattar* (the All-Veiling), *al-Bari* (the All-Holy Creator), and *al-Musawwir* (the All-Fashioning) are indicative of the manifestations of the Attribute of Making Exist on different wavelengths.

Whatever truth of the Divine Essence the Names reflect and whatever Attribute they translate, all of the All-Beautiful Names of God are expressive of a different beauty, sacredness, sanctity, and perfection in the name of that All-Transcending Being. Whenever they are mentioned, they mark the limits of the truths for belief with their meanings, contents, and luminosity, they arouse respect in believing spirits, and cause the hearts that beat with respect to turn to God once again, more deeply. Every blessed Name Which is mentioned in awareness in the depths of one's conscience removes the filth, soot, and rust from eyes and hearts, rips up the veils of corporeality, and shows spirits to the realms beyond and what lies further beyond. They remind us of the All-Sacred One to Whom they refer, as if they were our intercessors with Him; as long as people remember and mention God with these Names, hearts find contentment and rest. Furthermore, according to the rule, "The value of the knowledge is proportionate to what is known," those who know these blessed Names with respect to the Divine

Being and attain certain degrees of profundity through them are greatly valued by the inhabitants of the heavens and included in the candidates for the Divine Presence. If being a candidate for the Divine Presence depends on true knowledge of Him, then that All-Majestic, All-High Being can only be known with His Attributes of Majesty and Grace in the luminous atmosphere of these Names. We know things only according to the limited extent of our sensations of their corporeal beings, and judge them accordingly. But true knowledge about God Almighty with His all-transcending Existence can only be acquired by knowing the totality of all of His All-Beautiful Names; He can be known only beyond all modalities of quality and quantity. This reality also indicates that He is a Necessarily Existent Being Whose Existence is by Himself. This is what all Muslims believe.

Some scholars of Sufism and the Islamic creed have regarded the All-Beautiful Names as the foundation of the truths of the universe, things, and humanity. They have made a highly different interpretation of these Names, saying: "The truths of things consist in the Divine Names." According to them, all things, as well as all the willful and "instinctive" acts of humans and other beings—without ignoring the role of the free will in the acts of humans—are only mirrors that reflect the manifestations of the Divine Names. Bodies are only assemblages of material particles and compounds, while the Divine Names are in effect the spirits that reside in them. As for the true nature of these manifestations and the All-Majestic, All-High Divine Being Himself, before Whom the Names are veils, we should act in self-possession and remain in wonder, saying like the scholars of the *Ahlu's-Sunna*: "God is completely different from whatever comes to your mind concerning Him," or in the words of Imam ar-Rabbani: "God is beyond and further beyond whatever comes to your mind concerning Him." Even though certain impulses arise from feelings or fanciful attitudes, or, in the words of Imam al-Ghazzali, "the worldly reason or intellect" clouds our atmosphere of spirit and heart, we should try to remain within the limits of our creed, saying like Ziya Pasha:[103] "Perception of such transcendent matters is not something for our incapable reason / For these scales cannot measure such a great load."

If God Almighty had not introduced Himself to us with His All-Beautiful Names, we would never be able to comprehend the truth concerning these Names in what is going on in the universe or to know the All-Sacred Being Who is called by them. It is only through His making His Being, His Essential Characteristics, and His Attributes of Glory known that we are able to have knowledge of the truths that we know today, even though this is incomplete. It is our belief that the Names in question are the titles of His Being; as a result we try to acquire bits of knowledge about the truth of Divinity, voicing our requests at His Door, which is open to all, and constantly observe these Names in hopeful expectation that our requests will certainly be answered, provided we submit to His judgments and commands. We believe that we can overcome our various troubles and ailments and be saved from our centuries-old problems by turning to Him, using these Names, each of Which has the effect of a different mysterious medication, as intercessors with Him.

We approach the All-Beautiful Names and understand them in accordance with whatever meaning they have in God's sight and in the way the master of creation, upon him be the most perfect blessings and peace, perceived and interpreted them. We regard opposing considerations as deviance in thought and belief. How can we think and act otherwise when the Qur'an tells us that the denial of the Names, whether explicitly or by way of misguided interpretations, or the attribution of them, with their meanings and contents that are unique to God, to others than God is heresy? Declaring, *God—there is no deity save Him; His are the All-Beautiful Names* (20:8), the Qur'an refers the whole of existence, including human-

---

[103] Ziya Pasha (1825–1880) was one of the influential political and literary figures of the 19th century Ottoman Turkey. He published *Hurriya* (Freedom) newspaper. (Tr.)

kind and the universe with whatever occurs in it, to those All-Beautiful Names.

It is of great importance that every responsible person has recourse to the Divine Names so that they can have accurate knowledge of God and entreat Him properly and be able to establish a proper relationship with their Creator. We begin every good deed with His Names, and render every act of service under their supervision. We believe that any work done without having recourse to these will be fruitless. The Names *Allah* (God) and *ar-Rahman* (the All-Merciful) are of particular importance and have a special place in the Divine Being's sight. They are the first door through which we enter the clime of prayers and entreaties.

Even though some philosophers and the theologians influenced by them have put forward certain differing views about the All-Beautiful Names, as they have done for the Attributes, the scholars of the *Ahlu's-Sunna* have always acted with care, sensitivity, and self-possession. Without going into detail or useless interpretations, they have maintained that the Names can be identical to or separate from the Divine Essence. It has sometimes happened that they have asserted in a moderate style that the Names are neither identical to nor separate from the Divine Essence, thus preferring to distance themselves from further discussion.

Some others among the Sufis have opined that the All-Beautiful Names, Which we know and recite, are in fact the titles of the real Names, while the truth of Names lies beyond them. They have approached the matter of the Names, saying like Yunus Emre:[104] "There is Süleyman within Süleyman," and asserted that there is a relation between the Names we know and the real Divine Names that are behind existence which is similar to the relation between the corporeal heart and the spiritual heart and that which exists be-

---

[104] Yunus Emre (1240–1320). One of the most famous Sufi folk poets who have made a great impact on the Muslim-Turkish culture. His philosophy, metaphysics and humanism have been examined in various symposiums and conferences on a regular basis both in Turkey and abroad. (Tr.)

tween the spirit and the body. They have stressed that the real Names can only be realized through a profound spiritual experience and the ecstasy of feeling God's holy Presence.

No matter what their true nature is, the All-Beautiful Names Which God Almighty has taught us in his manifest Book are each a mysterious key for a certain sort of relationship with Him in the heart and the spirit; through these we can traverse our distance from Him, advancing toward nearness to Him, something that we are aware of in our conscience. They are each a mysterious word which gives an answer when spoken. Those who possess these keys and regularly recite these luminous words are not left unanswered even when they attempt to purchase all the worlds, and are not turned back with empty hands when they become customers for the realms beyond.

Experiencing and knowing the All-Beautiful Names with their own depths is a Divine favor for servants and a pleasure which will richen their spirits, and in respect of their outer and inner senses or faculties, it is an awareness of "seeing," knowing, and experiencing Him, and being seen and known by Him. Those who reach this horizon work for God's sake, begin every task for God's sake, and do whatever they do for God's sake; in the words of Bediüzzaman, they can make the seconds of their life as fruitful as the years of other people by moving and stopping "for God," "for God's sake," and "for the good pleasure of God." Why should this not be possible, as the servants are His servants, the Names are His Names, it is He Who is called by these Names, and the door to which the servants turn is His door?

* * *

Some scholars have asserted that God's Names are only those Which God and His Messenger have taught us as Divine Names, and it is not acceptable to derive Names from certain Divine Acts or to attribute them to God as being among His All-Beautiful Names. However, it is a fact that many Divine Acts are mentioned in the Qur'an in a way that will lead to different Names. Moreover, God Almighty has not taught us all of His Names. As our master, upon him be peace and blessings, stated in his prayer that begins with: "O God, I am Your servant, and the son of Your male servant, and the son of Your female servant,"[105] in addition to the All-Beautiful Names Which are mentioned in the Qur'an and certain Prophetic sayings, God has Names Which He mentioned in the previous Divine Books or Which He particularly informed some of His servants about or Which He keeps concealed with Him. However, we cannot know any of His Names unless He teaches them to us. We can know only the Names Which He has taught us either in the Qur'an or in the Sunna. Abu Hurayra, may God be pleased with him, narrates 99 Divine Names from the noblest Prophet, upon him be peace and blessings.[106] Even though these same Names are narrated from the Prophet by Salmanu'l-Farisi, 'Abdullah ibn 'Abbas, 'Abdullah ibn 'Umar, and Caliph 'Ali, may God be pleased with them, these narrations have not been authenticated. Some assert that the number 99 was used as a symbol of multiplicity in the *hadith* related by Abu Hurayra, therefore we cannot say that God's All-Beautiful Names are restricted to 99.

Those who have maintained that the All-Beautiful Names are only those which we have been taught by the Qur'an and the Sunna do not deem it proper to attribute any other Names to God Almighty. Furthermore, they do not approve of mentioning God with any names that do not seem to be in keeping with the Qur'anic concept of Divinity when used singly. Therefore, they tend to mention such Names as the All-Requiting, the One Who gives harm, and the All-Constricting together with certain other Names, such as the All-Glorious with irresistible might and the All-Requiting, the One Who gives harm and benefit, the All-Constricting and the All-Expanding. Based on the fact that physical causes have been established as veils before the Divine Power's involvement in insignificant-seeming affairs, it is possible to say that believers must always act in self-possession and with respect, care, and

---

105 Imam Malik, *al-Muwatta'*, "Jana'iz" 17; Ibn Hanbal, *al-Musnad*, 1:452.
106 *al-Bukhari*, "Shurut" 18; *Muslim*, "Dhikr" 5; *at-Tirmidhi*, "Da'awat" 82.

sensitivity with respect to how they approach the Divine Being. God is the Creator of everything, and therefore believers must mention Him as the Creator and avoid making specifications, such as the Creator of snakes or the Creator of vermin. However, we must also avoid going to the opposite extreme while taking care that nothing improper for God is attributed to him and claiming, like the *Mu'talizis*, that God does not create evil or ugly things or events. For it is He Who creates both good and evil, and a thing or event is evil not with respect to its creation, but with respect to its doer and cause. This attitude is required by both the necessity of considering God's Attributes correctly and observing the acts and effects of Divine Essential Characteristics, Attributes, and All-Beautiful Names. God is both the One of absolute grandeur and glory and the All-Merciful and All-Compassionate; He is both the All-Overwhelming and the All-Wise, both the One Severe in Punishment and the All-Patient. He is both the All-Majestic and the All-Gracious, and the All-Just and the All-Clement. We must always view Him in the light of the general meaning and content that is formed by the totality of His Attributes and Names.

The acts and designations attributed to God or mentioned in connection with Him must be considered from the perspective of His absolute Sacredness and Purity and His absolute exemption from any defect or resemblance to the created. For example, concepts such as making schemes, plotting, mocking, disgracing, or the like must be viewed and used in a style proper for the truth of Divinity and the essential characteristic of Divine Lordship. This is because respect for the Names and observing a style that is in keeping with God's absolute exemption from any defect or resemblance means being respectful for the All-Sacred One Who is called by these Names. Not only should the All-Beautiful Names be considered with appreciation and without imputing any faults or defects to them, also the Divine acts and all works or creatures of the Lord, which are mirrors, results, and the arena of the manifestations of these Names, must be treated the same on account of their being indicators or witnesses of God Almighty. Those who rightfully approach the matter from this perspective remind us of an important point: we must always be appreciative of Divine Acts, hold the Divine Names as being absolutely free from any defect, and exalt the All-Sacred Divine Being.

With respect to the level of existence of every thing and as it is something that has been created, every being, every object speaks of Him in its own peculiar language and style. All creatures say in unison:

> Our words differ, but Your Beauty is one;
> All of them indicate that All-Beautiful Face.

If a person can look at existence with their conscience and lend an ear to the messages of events, they will discern the reality expressed by Hoja Tahsin:

> Contemplate the lines of the universe,
> For they are missives to you from the Highest Realm.

How can this reality not be discerned seeing that His Being is, in one sense, announced through the lines of the universe, and His Knowledge, Life, Power, and Will are voiced through them, that the manifestations of His Names of Glory are known through them on different wavelengths, and everything gives us great joy and happiness through the most delicate embroideries of the subtlest art, order and harmony they display?

I should remind our readers once more that even though the most accurately narrated Tradition concerning the All-Beautiful Names is the one reported by Abu Hurayra, may God be pleased with him, according to the majority of scholars the Divine Names are not restricted to those mentioned in this Tradition. On the contrary, there are many other Divine Names that are mentioned in both the Qur'an and the Sunna, both explicitly and by allusion. The 99 blessed Names mentioned in the Tradition in question may have special importance in respect of prayers, entreaties, supplications, and particular instances of turning to God Almighty. For as mentioned above, there are other Names that certain other people have been informed of, but Which have not been disclosed to everyone. The number of Names Which are mentioned in the Qur'an and the books of the accurately related Prophetic Traditions in the forms of nouns, adjectives, and verbal nouns is as much as 550, and even reaches 1,000 in the Traditions related by members of the Prophet's Family.

In some cultures, God Almighty is mentioned with the Names or Titles Which are not opposed to the Qur'anic concept of the Divine Being, such as the One having no beginning, the Eternal in the past, the Eternal in the future, the Perpetual, the Everlasting, the Necessarily Existent Being, the Ever-Turner of hearts or the Ever-Disposer of hearts. "Tanrı" in Turkish and "Huda" in Persian can be viewed as being Names in the same strain. However, the promise for entering Paradise in return for consideration of God's Names seems to relate to the Tradition reported by Abu Hurayra. That is, it was promised that one would enter Paradise if they considered God's Names that were mentioned in the Prophetic Tradition reported by Abu Hurayra. We refer the truth of the matter to God Almighty; we turn to the scholars of Hadith for what is meant by consideration. They understand from this the regular, heart-felt recitation of those Names and the illumination of one's inner world through them, as well as being respectful for the concept of the Divine Being that arises from their totality, following the principles of good conduct they provide, and trying to be aware of the mysteries of Divinity expressed by them.

All of the All-Beautiful Names are absolutely sacred. Some have regarded it impermissible to use some of these Names for others than God. These are Names like *Allah* (God), *ar-Rahman* (the All-Merciful), *al-Quddus* (The All-Holy and All-Pure), *al-Muhyi*, (The Giver of Life and All-Reviving), *al-Mumit* (The One Who causes to die), *Maliku'l-Mulk* (The Absolute Master of all dominion), *Dhu'l-Jalali wa'l-Ikram* (The One of Majesty and Grace), *al-*

Akbar (The All-Great, the Greatest of All), *al-ʿAʿla* (The All-High), *al-Khaliq* (The Creator), *ʿAllamuʾl-Ghuyub* (The All-Knowing of the whole of the Unseen), and so on. If people want to give these Names to their children then they should add the word *ʿabd* (servant) before them. For example, they must use *ʿAbdullah* (God's servant), *ʿAbdur-Rahman* (the servant of the All-Merciful), and *ʿAbdul-Quddus* (the servant of the All-Holy and All-Pure). This knowledge of the Divine Names and this approach to both the Divine Names and the truths of Divinity are unique to the Muslim Community. This approach is exceptionally important, particularly in respect of reflecting the difference between the Creator and the created correctly; this is required by the Divinity as well as by the fact that God is the absolutely and exclusively All-Worshipped One. This is also our duty.

In fact, God's Essential, Affirmative, and Figurative Attributes and His Attributes of Exemption confirm this truth and call us to this correct approach. For this reason, in addition to knowing Him as the All-Knowing, the All-Living, the All-Powerful, the All-Hearing, the All-Seeing, the All-Willing, and the All-Speaking, based on their Affirmative Attributes, we must also affirm His absolute freedom from whatever is inappropriate for Divinity, such as impotence, poverty, neediness, defects, and having partners. Furthermore, we must in no way attribute any features that are peculiar to the created to God, such as being concerned with matter, time, space, physicality, or energy. We must believe that, in the words of Ibrahim Haqqi of Erzurum, God is an All-Majestic, All-High Being Who never eats or drinks, and Who is absolutely beyond time and space.

As will be mentioned below, some verifying scholars have divided the Divine Names into the categories such as the Names indicating the Divine Essence, the Names originating in the Affirmative Divine Attributes, and the Names indicating the Divine Acts. They have also regarded some Names as being the leaders or foundations of all the Names, and have made another categorization under the titles of the Names of Majesty and the Names of Grace. They have considered all the Names to be the foundation or source in which the truths of things originate or even these truths themselves, as well as being the means of all things being transferred from the Realm of the Unseen to the visible or manifest world through the Divine Knowledge, Wisdom, Will, and Power. Such scholars have stressed that these all-blessed Names are veils before the All-Sacred One Who is called by them. It is He alone Who knows the exact truth of everything, and what we must do is to believe in whatever He teaches us. It is unnecessary to make a detailed explanation of the All-Beautiful Names here as there are numerous studies that have been made so to date—a few of these were mentioned at the beginning of this article. You will find below the most widely known Divine Names only with just a brief explanation.

> O God! Show us the truth as the truth and enable us to live by it; show us falsehood as falsehood and enable us to avoid it. And bestow Your blessings and peace on our master Muhammad and on his Family and Companions, altogether.

The Names Indicating the Divine Essence

- *Allah:* God, the Proper Name of the Divine Being
- *(Ar-)Rabb*: The Lord (God as the Creator, Provider, Trainer, Upbringer, and Director of all creatures)
- *(Al-)Malik:* The All-Sovereign, The Owner and Master of everything
- *(Al-)Quddūs:* the All-Holy and All-Pure (Who is absolutely free of any defect)
- *(As-)Salam:* The Supreme Author of peace and salvation
- *(Al-)Mu'min:* The Supreme Author of safety and security
- *(Al-)Muhaymin:* The All-Watchful Guardian
- *(Al-)'Aziz*: The All-Glorious with irresistible might
- *(Al-)Jabbar:* The One Who manifests His Will and Grandeur

- *(Al-)Fard:* The All-Independent, Single One (free from having any equals or likes in His Essence and Attributes)
- *(Al-)Mutakabbir:* The One Who has exclusive right to all greatness and manifests it
- *(Al-)'Aliyy:* The All-Exalted
- *(Az-)Zahir:* The All-Outward, Whose existence is the most manifest
- *(Al-)Batin:* The All-Inward, Whose Essence cannot be comprehended
- *(Al-)Kabir:* The All-Great
- *(Al-)Jalil:* The All-Majestic and All-Supreme
- *(Al-)Majid:* The All-Sublime, the All-Illustrious
- *(Al-)Haqq:* The Ultimate Truth and Ever-Constant
- *(Al-)Matin:* The All-Forceful
- *(Al-)Wajid:* The Ever-Present and All-Finding
- *(As-)Samad:* The Eternally Besought, Himself being needy of nothing
- *(Al-)Awwal:* The First Whom there is none that precedes
- *(Al-)Akhir:* The Last Whom there is none that will outlive
- *(Al-)Muta'ali:* The All-Transcending
- *(Al-)Ghaniyy*: The All-Wealthy and Self-Sufficient
- *(An-)Nur:* The All-Light, Who is the unique source of all illumination
- *(Al-)Warith:* The One Who survives all beings and inherits them
- *Dhu'l-Jalal wa'l-ikram:* The One of absolute Majesty and Grace
- *(Ar-)Raqib:* The All-Watchful
- *(Al-)Baqi*: The Eternally All-Permanent
- *(Al-)Hamid*: The All-Praiseworthy
- *(Al-)Wahid*: The One of absolute Unity (Who is absolutely indivisible and having no partners and equals)

- *(Al-)Ahad*: The All-Unique of Absolute Oneness (Who is beyond all kinds of human conceptions and absolutely free from having any partners, likes, parents, sons or daughters)

THE NAMES ORIGINATING IN DIVINE ATTRIBUTES OF GLORY

- *(Al-)Hayy*: The All-Living
- *(Ash-)Shakur:* The All-Responsive (to the good and gratitude of His creatures)
- *(Al-)Qahhar*: The All-Overwhelming (with absolute sway over all that exists)
- *(Al-)Qahir:* The All-Overpowering, Who crushes those who deserve crushing
- *(Al-)Muqtadir:* The All-Omnipotent
- *(Al-)Qawiyy:* The All-Strong
- *(Al-)Murid:* The All-Willing
- *(Al-)Qadir:* The All-Powerful
- *(Ar-)Rahman:* The All-Merciful (Who has mercy on the whole of existence and provides for all of them)
- *(Ar-)Rahim*: The All-Compassionate (Who has particular compassion for each of His creatures in their maintenance, and for His believing servants especially in the other world)
- *(As-)Subhan:* The All-Glorified
- *(As-)Sultan:* The Absolute, Eternal Authority
- *(Al-)Karim:* The All-Munificent
- *(Al-)Ghaffar:* The Oft-Forgiver of sins
- *(Al-)Ghafur:* The All-Forgiving
- *(Al-)Wadud:* The All-Loving and All-Beloved
- *(Ar-)Rauf:* The All-Pitying
- *(Al-)Halim:* The All-Clement (showing no haste to punish the errors of His servants)
- *(Al-)Barr:* The All-Benign

- *(As-)Sabur:* The All-Patient (Whom no haste induces to rush into an action)
- *(Al-)'Alim:* The All-Knowing
- *(Al-)Khabir:* The All-Aware
- *(Al-)Muhsi:* The All-Counting and Recording
- *(Al-)Hakim:* The One Who does everything properly, the All-Wise
- *(Ash-)Shahid:* The All-Witnessing
- *(As-)Sami':* The All-Hearing
- *(Al-)Basir:* The All-Seeing
- *(Al-)'Afuww*: The All-Pardoning (Who overlooks the faults of His servants and grants remission)

THE NAMES INDICATING DIVINE ACTS

- *(Al-)Mubdi:* The All-Initiating
- *(Al-)Wakil*: The One to rely on and to Whom affairs should be entrusted
- *(Al-)Baith:* The One Who restores life to the dead
- *(Al-)Mujib:* The All-Answering (of prayers) and Meeting (of needs)
- *(Al-)Wasi'*: The All-Embracing (in His Knowledge and Mercy)
- *(Al-)Hasib*: The All-Sufficing as One Who reckons and settles the accounts (of His servants)
- *(Al-)Mughis*: The One Who gives extra help
- *(Al-)Hafiz*: The All-Preserving and Keeper of records, the All-Protecting
- *(Al-)Khaliq*: The Creator (Who determines measure for everything and makes things and beings exist out of nothing)
- *(as-)Sani'*: The Maker

- *(Al-)Bari*: The All-Holy Creator (Who is absolutely free from having any partners and Who creates without imitating anything)
- *(Al-)Musawwir*: The All-Fashioning
- *(Ar-)Razzaq*: The All-Providing
- *(Al-)Wahhab*: The All-Bestowing
- *(As-)Sattar*: The All-Veiling (of His servants' shortcomings and sins)
- *(Al-)Fatir*: The All-Originating (with a unique individuality)
- *(Al-)Fattah*: The One Who opens the door of good
- *(An-)Nasir*: The All-Helping and Giver of Victory
- *(Al-)Kafi*: The All-Sufficing
- *(Al-)Qabid*: The All-Constricting; the One Who takes the souls of living beings
- *(Al-)Basit*: The All-Expanding
- *(Al-)Hafid*: The One Who lowers and humiliates whom He wills
- *(Ar-)Rafiʿ*: The All-Elevating
- *(Al-)Muʿizz*: The All-Exalting and Honoring
- *(Al-)Mudhill*: The All-Abasing
- *(Al-)Hakam*: The All-Judging (Who settles the matters between people)
- *(Al-)ʿAdl*: The All-Just
- *(Al-)Latif*: The All-Subtle (penetrating into the minutest dimensions of all things and providing for all)
- *(Al-)Muʿid*: The All-Returning and Restoring (the One Who causes to die after life and returns the dead to life)
- *(Al-)Muhyi*: The Giver of life and All-Reviving
- *(Al-)Mumit*: The One Who causes to die; the All-Dealing of death
- *(Al-)Waliyy*: The Guardian, the Protecting Friend (to rely on)

- *(At-)Tawwab*: The One Who guides to repentance, accepts repentance, and returns it with liberal forgiveness and additional reward
- *(Al-)Muntaqim*: The Ever-Able to requite
- *(Al-)Muqsit*: The All-Dealing of justice
- *(Al-)Jamiʿ*: The One having all excellences to the infinite degree; the All-Gathering
- *(Al-)Mughni*: The All-Enriching
- *(Al-)Maniʿ*: The All-Preventing and Withdrawing; the One Who does not give whatever He does not will to give
- *(Ad-)Darr*: The Creator of evil and harm
- *(An-)Nafiʿ*: The All-Favoring and Giver of benefits
- *(Al-)Hadi*: The All-Guiding
- *(Al-)Badiʿ*: The One Who originates in unique fashion and with nothing preceding Him to imitate
- *(Ar-)Rashid*: The All-Guide to what is correct
- *(Al-)Qayyūm*: The Self-Subsistent (by Whom all subsist)
- *Maliku'l-mulk*: The absolute Master of all dominion
- *(Al-)Muʿakhkhir*: The One Who leaves behind
- *(Al-)Muqaddim*: The One Who causes to advance, Who moves things forward
- *(Al-)Muqit*: The All-Aiding and Sustaining
- *(al-)Wali*: The All-Governing

The Foundational Names

- *(Al-)Hayy*: The All-Living
- *(Al-)ʿAlim*: The All-Knowing
- *(Al-)Murid*: The All-Willing
- *(Al-)Mutakallim*: The All-Speaking
- *(Al-)Qadir*: The All-Powerful
- *(Al-)Jawad*: The All-Generous
- *(Al-)Muqsit*: The One Who judges with justice

The Names of Majesty

- *(Al-)Kabir:* The All-Great
- *(Al-)'Aziz:* The All-Glorious with irresistible might
- *(Al-)'Alim:* The All-Knowing
- *(Al-)Jalil:* The All-Majestic and All-Supreme
- *(Ad-)Dayyan:* The Supreme Ruler and All-Requiting (of good and evil)
- *(Al-)Majid:* The All-Sublime, the All-Illustrious
- *(Al-)Mumit:* The One Who causes to die; the All-Dealing of death
- *(Ad-)Darr:* The Creator of evil and harm
- *(Al-)Muntaqim:* The All-Requiting

The Names of Grace

- *(Ar-)Rahim:* The All-Compassionate (Who has particular compassion for each of His creatures in their maintenance, and for His believing servants especially in the other world)
- *(Al-)Jamil:* The All-Gracious and All-Beautiful
- *(As-)Salam:* The Supreme Author of peace and salvation
- *(Al-)Muhyi:* The Giver of life and All-Reviving
- *(Al-)Mu'min:* The Supreme Author of safety and security
- *(Al-)Latif:* The All-Subtle (penetrating into the minutest dimensions of all things and providing for all)
- *(Ar-)Razzaq:* The All-Providing
- *(Al-)Khallaq:* The Supreme Creator
- *(Al-)Awwal:* The First (Whom there is none that precedes)
- *(Al-)Akhir:* The Last (Whom there is none that will outlive)
- *(Az-)Zahir:* The All-Outward, Whose existence is the most manifest
- *(Al-)Batin:* The All-Inward, Whose Essence cannot be comprehended
- *(Al-)Qarib:* The All-Near

PUTTING AN END TO A LONG JOURNEY

Human beings are exceptional creatures in creation; they are travelers whose journey of life passes through the Realm of the Transcendental Manifestation of Divine Commands; their eyes are fixed on the Realm of the Transcendental Manifestation of Divine Attributes and Names, and they intend to advance as far as the Realm of the Transcendental Manifestation of Divinity. Human beings are the falcons of the realm of corporeality and are equipped with a great capacity that is open to extra developments and gifts. They begin their journey from the realm of spirits, stop for some time in this abode of troubles and bounties, known as the realm of corporeality or the manifest or physical realm and regarded as a cloudy mirror of the Realm of the Transcendental Manifestation of Divine Commands, and during their temporary stay in this guesthouse, with respect to their insight and horizon of heart, they live turned to the Realm of the Transcendental Manifestation of Divine Attributes and Names, which is the real source of light. While looking up toward the peaks of the Realm of the Transcendental Manifestation of Divine Attributes and Names from the horizon of these Names and Attributes, they dream of the Realm of the Transcendental Manifestation of Divinity, tasting the pleasure of different observations with dreams of advancing farther and farther, and progress toward the final point of nearness toward God, which each can attain according to their particular capacity. With their free will absolutely submitted to God's Will and their outer and inner eyes fixed on the highway of the Prophets, the truthful ones who are completely loyal to God's Path, and the pious, righteous, endeavoring to please God with every act, aware of the subtle meaning of obedience to the Creator, and under the guidance of the noblest Messenger, upon him be peace and blessings, with, they walk toward the realms beyond the heavens, searching for new knowledge about God from everybody and everything they pass. They shudder at the mention of "He!" along the path and push themselves further and further ahead at full speed, like fiery steeds, at the mention of their All-Worshipped, All-Besought, All-Loved One.

The noble Shari'a is a constantly true guide that never misleads, and the styles that allow different interpretations in the two basic sources of the Shari'a—the Qur'an and the Sunna—and are regarded as the manifestations of Divine Mercy on different wavelengths, are special gifts and blessings for different temperaments and dispositions and unique breezes from the realms beyond which take the travelers to different depths. The love of truth is an inexhaustible source of energy in the spirit, and the sounds and voices that are heard everywhere, the different tunes and melodies, and the decorative beauty observed everywhere are all messages of knowledge about God and the voices of truth. These pour into the valleys of the faculties of the travelers and it is through these gifts, wrapped one within the other, that the *Shari'a, tariqa* (spiritual discipline), *ma'rifa* (knowledge of God) and *haqiqa* (truth) appear as dimensions of the same fundamental truth; despite each having its own basic principles, they are in perfect harmony with one another.

For those who are looking from this horizon, different states, attributes, acts, and events are indicators of different Divine Names, and the witnesses of God, the Ultimate Truth, are manifest everywhere. Human faculties deepen in their sensations, and the "archetypes," which are regarded as the background of existence, begin to be perceived. The Divine Attributes, upon Which Divine Names are based, manifest themselves at certain degrees according to the capacity of each traveler; thus, continuous dewdrops begin to descend onto the slopes of hearts from the horizon of the Absolute Identity. This happens until the Divine faculty or intellectual heart is able to contemplate the Unity of the Divine Essence and saved from self-consideration; the result is that it goes into ecstasies. If the limit of such a one who has reached the end of the spiritual journey extends as high as the horizon of the Perfect or Universal Man, the detailed becomes observed in the brief and the brief becomes perceived and experienced in the detailed. The breezes of sensation and perception pervade everywhere and are felt on different wavelengths of manifestation, according to the capacity of each traveler; the slopes of hearts are covered with showers of a variety of gifts. There are as many ways of perception and experience as the number of hearts and as many methods or systems as the breaths of creatures. In such an atmosphere one can be protected against confusions only by strictly following the way of Muhammad, upon him be peace and blessings.

It is by means of these methods that the travelers to the Ultimate Truth are able to cover the distance that separates them from God and begin to be aware of His nearness by "journeying toward Him" on the horizon of their hearts and spirits; they remove their selves from between them and God in the stage of "journeying in God" and try to obey Him and please Him in all their thoughts, sayings, and actions. They attempt to transcend their selves to experience His company through the favor of "journeying with God" and at the stage of "journeying from God," they are enraptured with the enthusiasm of causing others to feel what they have felt, to attain what they have attained, and to know what they have known. They put the color of unity on multiplicity, running to make that Most Manifest One known by all, always mentioning Him wherever they are and whenever they have an opportunity. In my opinion, this is the purpose of being a true human being.

A spirit which journeys around this horizon utters "God" with every breath and breathes "He!" in every second of their life; such a one utters, like Ismail Haqqi, and breathes "He!":

> The mention of He is the source of life itself
> and the soul for the body;

The mention of He is the fountain that sends water
descending into the garden of youth.
It is He Who makes manifest and Who manifests
Himself in eighteen thousand worlds;
The mention of He is a gift for all whose
eye of soul is receptive.
The gems of mysteries are extracted from
the mine of the meaning of He;
Only one with knowledge of God knows
what glory the mention of He is.
Spend your capital of life on the mention of He
at night and in daytime,
For the perfect prosperity and the most
loyal friend is the mention of He.

·····

It is the sun of the mention of He which fills
the tongues with light;
O Haqqi, it is the mention of He that
every particle constantly busies itself with.

Such heroes of belief in Divine Unity as these turn round the
fountains of repentance, penitence, and contrition so that they are
completely purified of all sins and faults; they avoid affectation in
their spiritual states and experiences, constantly breathing with fear
and awe of God. They try to lead an extremely simple, austere life
in accordance with the rule: "Let your burden be light, for the hill
to climb is steep and high," while doing their utmost to spend
their life in the greenhouses of piety, righteousness, and absti-
nence. They adopt trust in God, utmost reliance on Him, and submission and commitment to Him as the sole source of their
strength. They scrutinize and criticize themselves many times a day
for even the slightest of lapses, pulling themselves together through
a shower of Divine gifts. They greet God's bounties with thanks-
giving, renew their heartfelt resignation to God's judgments and
decrees in the face of trials, and tremble with fear that the bounties arriving without having been asked for may be a cause of perdition. They never pursue any spiritual pleasures or wonderwork-

ing, never contaminate their minds or tongues with foul language, as if they are putting their enthusiasms and breaths under the control of the realms beyond and further beyond. They never abandon truthfulness even at the cost of their own lives, and accept good manners and modesty as "the garment of piety and righteousness," trying to live in utmost chastity like angels. They are aware that sincerity and purity of intention must be the spirit of whatever they do, and without this their actions are not acceptable in God's sight. They regard generosity and magnanimity as a requirement of being human and always act in the spirit of altruism, trying to repel evil with good and never leaving any good done to them without return. Thus, their spiritual life gains new depths every day through self-supervision and self-criticism. They admit that their innate impotence and poverty are true means of reaching the Absolutely Wealthy and Powerful One. They see the gifts coming to them as bounties that they have never deserved, and they are filled with gratitude.

Representing the good morals or virtues and voicing the spirit of the Qur'an are the "natural" state of those profound spirits that are dedicated to gaining God's approval and good pleasure. Weighing each of their acts on the scales of excellence or always acting as if seeing God or in awareness of God's always seeing them has become their unchanging nature. Out of His pure grace, God has created them with the capacity of attaining this degree of spirituality because He knew beforehand that they would use their free will to the fullest in order to attain such a state. They are so sincerely religious that it is the spirit of the Religion and heavenliness that are always manifested in their every action, as well as in their treatment of people and their interpretation of existence. Religious life is their unchanging character, and the Prophet, upon him be the perfect blessings and peace, is their guide in both worlds, while knowledge of God is their provision in their worldly travel, and the love of truth is the true color of their aims and pursuits. They are clean to the utmost degree, both physically and spiritually. Their hearts are always open to the truth and the Truth of truths, as if the brightest of mirrors; their worlds of the spirit and secrets are like telescopes that are turned toward the realms beyond and further beyond. They try to seek and find whatever can be seen and they cause original compositions of different sounds and voices to be heard.

Despite their richness in Divine gifts and profundity, such people are extraordinarily modest and humble, and in a continuous struggle with arrogance and haughtiness. They are so determined against whatever displeases God that even if all human beings came together to force them to do anything displeasing to God, they would refrain from doing it. They constantly observe the realms beyond the horizon with their outer and inner eyes and spend their lives in self-possession, as if they were always in Prayer. They continuously breathe with love of and yearning for God and are ever ready to sacrifice their souls for the sake of their All-Beloved. Renouncing everything worldly, no matter how valuable it might be in the sight of others, they submit themselves wholly to Him as if a they were a corpse placed on the stone for the funeral Prayer, pronouncing His Grandeur and Exaltedness, condemning themselves to nothingness. How beautiful is the following couplet by Hafiz:[107]

> When I took ablution at the fountain of love,
> I pronounced the Grandeur of God
> four times over whatever I had.

The Sufis have expressed this same idea as follows: "When one takes ablution at the fountain of love, they then regard the world, the other world, and themselves as dead, thus pronouncing God's Grandeur four times as if performing the funeral Prayer; anyone who has not done so has not turned in the direction (*qibla*) to which they must turn." Unless one can abandon all of existence on account of itself, they will not be able to turn to God per-

---

[107] Hafiz al-Shirazi (1230–1291) is the greatest lyric poet of Persia, who took the poetic form of *ghazal* to unparalleled heights of subtlety and beauty. (Tr.)

fectly. Unless one is not filled with feelings of regard, appreciation, love, sincere relationship and friendship, and is not completely saved from consideration of others than God to attain perfect purity by having no expectations other than God's good pleasure, they will not be able to attain the special horizon of turning completely to Him. It should first of all be recognized that one who has not turned to God will not be able to receive regard or attention from Him. Even though those who lack feelings of appreciation live long, they are not regarded as having really lived. The bosoms that are devoid of love are no different from ruins that are not worth seeing. The sincere relationship with the true Friend grows only on the ground of love for God. The status of His sincere friendship is a special favor for those who have assigned their hearts to the most sincere Friend, and Divine favors and gifts are among the surprises that are at times offered to those who have dedicated themselves to gaining the approval and good pleasure of the Ultimate Truth.

The Divine Being's regard, attention, and mercy for human beings are in keeping with His infinitude, while the regard and attention given by humans to Him are in proportion to their restricted capacities. Broadening this restricted capacity in the face of that infinitude is dependent on the servants' purity of intention, faithfulness, loyalty, and sincerity. It sometimes occurs that Divine help, favor, and protection are manifested according to the vastness of His Mercy, due to which Divine regard and attention turn drops of water into seas and particles into the sun. For this reason, however one turns to God, He will not allow those who turn to His Door to suffer loss or disillusionment. He does not abandon those who follow His commands to the pitilessness of the paths, nor does He deprive those who are traveling toward knowledge of Him of His companionship. Sometimes He even gives enough value to a single drop of resolution and endeavor that has been put forth with purity of intention and sincerity to gain the Gardens of Paradise. He makes an iota of belief and knowledge of God the means of salvation and grants a kingdom to the servants waiting at His Door.

Those who have walked toward God without swerving have never been obstructed. None among those who have mentioned Him sincerely in their hearts has ever suffered loss or disappointment. None among those who have set off toward Him with purity of intention has been condemned to eternal loss. Some have always been aware of God in the depths of their hearts, owing to a slight tendency toward Him to fulfil the right of the willpower with which they have been equipped; some have risen to the lofty station at which "kings" are crowned in return for a determined decision to do some good in the future. Still others have advanced so far as to be established on the throne of sincere friendship with God in response for the sensitivity that they have shown in carrying out the religious commands, while some have used their sagacity, insight, intelligence, and logic to an optimum degree, thus attaining true knowledge of God in a single attempt. There are others who have advanced so far as to be able to reach the "shadow of God" without encountering any opposing wind, because they have spent their life in the greenhouses of chastity, innocence, and modesty. Others have aimed to take "the ten steps" one after the other and thus attain the heroism of resolution, steadfastness, and utmost sensitivity when carrying out their religious duties, while others have divided this long, narrow path into seven parts, reaching the horizon of receiving God's special attention and regard by means of the special help that comes to the weary traveler in subtle ways. Still others have adopted the principle, "Poverty is my pride," and have become as selfless as a dewdrop that is ready to be evaporated by a ray of the sun and thus feel the Eternal Sun in its pupil, acting in constant expectation of God's company. Still others have based their journey on the principles of the admission of one's innate impotence and poverty before God and enthusiasm and thankfulness, always pouring out their hearts to Him with songs of compassion on the plains of reflective thought, continuously uttering "He!" in the bright clime of signposts. Yet others have strictly followed the elevated, good conduct of Ahmad, upon him be peace and blessings, on the horizon of life that is lived at the level of the heart and spirit, and have been fed by the gifts that pour down on his table... In short, everyone who has set off to reach God sincerely has continuously advanced toward Him by following a different path or system, which indicates the infinitude of Divine Mercy and marks a different manifestation of Divine regard for different temperaments and dispositions; they try to cover the distance that lays between God and those seeking God according to their knowledge of Him.

Some among these travelers have done their utmost to attain what they have intended, displaying or offering most beautiful examples to follow and entrusting their experiences to the insight of others, while others have preferred to groan with the pen and pour themselves out with ink, clothing their spiritual states with written expressions, thus providing the possibility to follow behind to those who will come later. Both of these groups have acted correctly; it is not only the right of these heroes of spirituality to receive respect from us, it is also our duty to pay respect to them.

In *Emerald Hills of the Heart*, we have tried to deal with some of the embroideries of the spiritual state and pleasure, the overflowing ecstasy, rapture and excitement, and the gems of word and meaning, which have so far been experienced, spoken, and embroidered on the pages of books, and present them from our own horizon. We have sometimes observed them from afar on their own horizon and have tried to picture them according to the capacities of the spiritual receptors, referring the truth of the matter to the All-Knowing of the whole Unseen. What we have written is the description of spiritual states and pleasures. Any such state or pleasure can only be experienced and it is not possible for those who cannot experience them to recognize such states in all their depths. All spoken and written words concerning these states are only shadows of what has been reflected from the breast. The original is always different from the shadow. A spiritual state and pleasure is one thing, while description of it is something else. For example, modesty reflects itself in all acts of a human being who has this characteristic; we can only perceive modesty from afar through certain traces. Sincerity or purity of intention is the spirit of actions and—in the words of some of God's friends—the wing of the bird of worship and obedience. It is only God Who knows the truth of this, even though some heroes of insight can perceive it to a certain degree. Even though everyone knows that spiritual pleasure, enthusiasm, and contentment are the fruits of the horizon of belief, Islamic life, and excellence in actions, only the heroes of austerities who have overcome their corporeality can understand the depth contained therein. It demonstrates one's sincerity in worship, submission, and deep devotion to God that one does not exult because of what has been granted to them, nor does one grieve for what has been missed. One should refuse, even become irritated by, any praise, and not be annoyed by criticism; one should distance themselves from sins in the same way that they distance themselves from snakes and vermin, fulfilling their duties of worship in good and high spirits, as if they were about to meet with God. However, those who do not pursue perfection, precision, or completion cannot understand this.

Fear and awe of God, and deep reverence are the states of those who have attained a certain degree of certainty and true knowledge of God. Even though those who are lacking in knowledge and spiritual understanding of God cannot comprehend much of such things, the heroes of certainty are well aware of them, and tremble, whether with fear or awe or deep reverence, yet always giving the impression that they are in God's Presence. Referring everything good or bad to God's final judgment and relying and depending on Him are special gifts that are given in return for perfect belief, while those who do not respond to God's judgments or decisions with perfect submission and resignation and who do not see their endeavors as only a petition to God's Will can never be saved from throwing stones at Destiny; such people always accuse others, and are never willing to agree to criticize themselves. One who has not been able to make their inner world into a honeycomb of belief, and knowledge and love of God is unaware of the love and the meaning of tears. Such people live all their lives bereft of or wearied of pursuing excitement and emotions and can never feel the deep spiritual pleasure of pouring themselves out to God in a solitary corner with sighs and tears. Even though it has been witnessed that such crude souls weep, their weeping resembles the weeping of children whose toys have been taken from their hands. Weeping is, in fact, the voice or translation of the purity of spirit and tenderheartedness. Human faculties are stirred up by this voice, and the slopes of the heart begin to green; spring arrives in the human world of emotions. How well expressed are the following words of Mawlana Jalalu'd-Din ar-Rumi:

> If clouds were not to weep, the grass would not smile; if infants were not to weep, the milk would not flow; you should know that unless there is weeping, the Lord of the lords does not give milk.

Some of God's friends say in the same strain: "Those who do not weep today will not be able to be saved from sighing and mourning tomorrow." This must have been said in accordance with the Prophetic supplication, "O God! I seek refuge in You from eyes that do not weep."[108]

It is not possible for one who does not believe to have true knowledge of God; a breast devoid of knowledge of God cannot have Divine excitement, and a spirit bereft of such excitement cannot shed tears from love or yearning for or fear and awe of God. The most important grounds for the feeling of fear and awe of God is *taqwa*, which means piety, righteousness, and deep reverence for God and seeking refuge in His protection. To explain this better, *taqwa* consists of heeding and carrying out God's religious com-

---

[108] Ibn Hajar al-Asqalani, *Fathu'l-Bari*, 11:139.

mands, thus deepening one's theoretical belief through worship and deep devotion. *Taqwa* also consists of traveling through or studying "natural" phenomena and reading, feeling, sensing, and recognizing God in the face of everything and every event, thus always trying to increase in certainty, advancing toward Him through steps of nearness to Him, and thus living a deeper life by His company.

Taqwa is a safe highway that extends toward love of God and His approval and good pleasure; thus it is the primary foundation of being truly human in God's sight. It is a way of getting near to Him, the ticket or document for traveling the path that leads to meeting with Him, the food and water of the other life, and the certificate that saves one from Hell and allows entrance to Paradise. The one who has attained *taqwa* and deepened in it as a dimension of their life has obtained the most precious treasure with which to "purchase" a mansion in the other world. Every door knocked on with sighs of *taqwa* will certainly be opened tomorrow, if not today; the ways of the hearts that beat with a feeling of *taqwa* are illuminated by lights from the realms beyond. Consider that in the manifest Qur'an, God Almighty has made guidance to the Straight Path and salvation in the other world dependent on it. To express this, a friend of God wrote:

> God Almighty says: "The great among you are those
> who are God-revering, pious.
> The last abode of the God-revering, pious ones
> will be Paradise and their drink will be *kawthar*."

We cannot say that we have comprehended *taqwa* with its place in God's sight and with all that it promises. I have neither been able to comprehend nor explain it. I have lowered it below from its heavenly horizon and presented it in the narrowness of my capacity of perception and description. Who knows what other heavenly truths like *taqwa* I have transformed into earthly concepts due to my limited ability. However, if the highest level of *taqwa* is, according to some, remaining distant from everything which will contaminate the spirit, keeping silent in any matter that is not pleasing to God, avoidance of even any image or conception in opposition to God's decrees, always pursuing His good pleasure and living with the intention of feeling, seeing, and knowing Him only and attaining His company, and always breathing with Him with the mention of "He!" in utter oblivion of one own self—if *taqwa* consist of all these, then it is beyond our capacity of perception or description. Those who experience it at this level travel and live in the realms that are beyond any dimensions we know, saying:

> The lights of my eyes are "He!", and
> the decree guiding my intellect is "He!"
> The utterance of my tongue is "He!" and
> what is manifested from my wailings is "He!
> The recreation of my heart is "He!"
> and the beloved of my soul is "He!"
>
> ....
>
> Its fasting is "He!", its festival is "He!",
> and its abstinence and piety are "He!"
> Its meeting with God is "He!", its separation is "He!",
> and the remedy for its ailments is "He!"

As for me, I can only approach and describe it according to my capacity of perception and on the map of my spirit.

There are some other states like excellence in worship and other states and actions even beyond excellence such as always living in awareness of God's omnipresence and uninterruptedly pursuing the truths that cannot be attained through eyes or other external senses, not even through the mind. People like me either keep silent concerning these or lend ears to those who are qualified to talk about them, only making conjectures. Those who attain these states observe many truths that are hidden to others, scattering around many ever-original gems from the treasures of the Unseen, and offering those who follow them exquisite things from among the Divine gifts that are given to them as presents for their insight. A hero of such a degree of ecstasy and immersion gives voice to his boiling feelings as follows:

> The Beautiful One has once more shown me His Face
> from His Palace of Majesty;
> I am once more a wailing, mad lover intoxicated
> with the eternal wine;
> The veil of ignorance has once more been removed
> from my eyes and heart;
> A call has come to my soul from among the calls of
> the All-Transcending One.
>
> Yazıcızade[109]

In *Emerald Hills of the Heart*, we have tried to sometimes picture what we have heard from the specialists concerning this multicolored map, sometimes that which we have attained and perceived from relevant books or booklets, sometimes that which we have read on the faces of certain happenings which are common and legendary, and sometimes what has been experienced, spoken, or reported through ages—we have tried to picture these and say some things in the name of the provision and the principles of the journey of the luminous travelers of the Sufi path.

It would be an exaggeration to say that we have been able to interpret according to the Book (the Qur'an) and the Sunna whatever has been said concerning the matters discussed. However, I would like to say that I have done my best and acted with great sensitivity so as to be able to interpret every approach and consideration according to these two basic sources of Islam. The tears I have many times shed over the black lines, which I regard as my sins of thinking, are witnesses to this. I have many times trembled with the consideration that I have not been able to present the elevated, transcending truths in accordance with their essential reality

---

[109] Yazıcızade Muhammed Efendi (d. 1451). One of the important Sufi and literary figures in the 15th century Ottoman Turkey. He lived in Gallipoli. *Muhammediye*, which is about the life and excellencies of the Prophet Muhammad, is his most famous work. (Tr.)

or real nature, and have nearly decided to give up continuing to write about them. I must admit that I have had difficulties in finding religiously true bases for some ambiguous utterances of people of deep spirituality—statements that are apparently incompatible with the essentials of the Religion—or in conforming perfectly to the unique place of the Religion in God's sight and the fact that the people of deep spirituality are the living representatives of it. I have continuously shuddered with the fear that while trying to remain respectful for the transcending position of the truth and the Ultimate Truth of the truths, I have not been able to explain relevant matters in accordance with their original, essential reality or true nature.

I cannot claim that whatever I have written is true. It is God Almighty Who knows the exact truth of everything. If all that I have written and done is the expression of the truth and has been written and done with the intention of pleasing God, it is from Him and by Him; while whatever mistake has been made, even though I have intended God's approval and reward, any failure in the pursuit of God's good pleasure, is from me. I seek refuge in my Lord with the excuse and veil that "All children of Adam are subject to erring much, and the best of those who err much are the oft-repentant,"[110] and request that God also open for me the door of repentance and contrition, a door that He has opened for those who have come before me.

---

[110] at-Tirmidhi, Qiyama, 49; Ibn Maja, "Zuhd" 30.

BIBLIOGRAPHY

'Abdu'Razzaq, Abu Bakr 'Abdu'Razzaq ibn Hammam, *al-Musannaf*, I–IX, al-Majlisu'l-'Ilmi, Beirut, 1983.

Abu Dawud, Sulayman ibn Ash'as as-Sijistani, *as-Sunan*, I–II, Daru'l-Jinan, Beirut, 1988.

Abu Nu'aym, Ahmad ibn 'Abdillah al-Isbahani, *Hilyatu'l-Awliya wa Tabaqatu'l-Asfiya*, I–IX, Daru'l-Kutubi'l-'Ilmiyya, Beirut, 1988.

Abu Talib al-Makki, Muhammad ibn 'Ali ibn 'Atiyya, *Qutu'l-Qulub fi Mu'malati'l-Mahbub wa Wasfi Tariqi'l-Muridi ila Maqami't-Tawhid*, Daru'-Sadr, Beirut, 1995.

Abu Ya'la, Ahmad ibn 'Ali al-Musanna, *al-Musnad*, I–XIII, Daru'l-Ma'mun li't-Turath, Damascus, 1984.

Ahmad ibn Hanbal, Abu 'Abdullah ash-Shaybani, *al-Musnad*, I–IV, al-Maktabatu'l-Islami, Beirut, 1993.

(al-)'Ajluni, Isma'il ibn Muhammad, *Kashfu'l-Khafa' wa Muzilu'l-Ilbas*, I–II, Muassatu'r-Risala, Beirut, 1986.

'Aliyyu'y-Qari, 'Ali ibn Sultan Muhammad al-Harawi, *al-Masnu'*, Maktabatu'r-Rushd, Riyad, 1985.

——, *al-Asraru'l-Marfu'a fi Abhari'l-Mawdu'a*, al-Maktabatu'l-Islami, Beirut, 1987.

(al-)Alusi, Abu's-Sana Shihabu'd-Din Mahmud ibn 'Abdillah, *Ruhu'l-Ma'ani fi Tafsiri'l-Qur'ani'l-'Azim wa's-Sab'ul-Mathani*, I–XXX, Daru Ihyai't-Turathi'l-'Arabi, Beirut.

(al-)Baghdadi, al-Khatib Abu Bakr Ahmad ibn Thabit, *Tarikhu Baghdad aw Madinatu's-Salam*, I–XIX, Daru'l-Kutubi'l-'Ilmiyya, Beirut.

(al-)Bayhaqi, Abu Bakr Ahmad ibn Husayn, *as-Sunanu'l-Kubra*, I–IX, Maktabatu Dari'l-Baz, Makka, 1994.

——, *Shu'abu'l-Iman*, I–VIII, Daru'l-Kutubi'l-'Ilmiyya, Beirut, 1990.

(al-)Bukhari, Abu 'Abdillah Muhammad ibn Isma'il, *Sahihu'l-Bukhari*, I–VIII, Daru'l-Kutubi'l-'Ilmiyya, Beirut, 1994.

Bursavi, Ismail Haqqi, *Tafsiru Ruhi'l-Bayan*, I–X, Maktabatu'l-Islamiya, 1330 AH / 1911 CE.

(ad-)Darimi, 'Abdullah ibn 'Abdur-Rahman, *as-Sunan,* I–II, Daru'l-Qalam, Beirut, 1991.

Erzurumi, Ibrahim Haqqi, *Marifetname*, Istanbul, 1300 [Ottoman Rumi calendar] / 1885 CE.

(al-)Ghazali, Imam Abu Hamid Muhammad, *Ihya'u 'Ulumi'd-Din*, I–IV, Daru'l-Ma'rifa, Beirut.

——, *al-Maqsadu'l-Athna fi Sharhi Ma'ani'i Asma'illahi'l-Husna*, al-Jifan wa'l-Jabi, Cyprus.

(al-)Hakim, Abu 'Abdillah Muhammad ibn 'Abdillah al-Naysaburi, *al-Mustadrak ala's-Sahihayn*, I–IV, Daru'l-Kutubi'l-'Ilmiyya, Beirut, 1990.

Ibn Hajar, Abu'l-Fadl Shahabu'd-Din Ahmad al-Asqalani, *Fathu'l-Bari fi Shrah-i Sahihi'l-Bukhari*, I–XIII, Daru'l-Ma'rifa, Beirut.

Ibn Hibban, Abu Hatim Muhammad al-Busti, *al-Ihsan fi Takrib-i Sahihi ibn Hibban*, Muassatu'r-Risala, Beirut, 1988.

Ibnu'l-'Arabi, Muhyi'd-Din, *al-Futuhatu'l-Makkiya*, I–IV. Beirut, n.d.

Ibn Kathir, Abu'l-Fida Isma'il ibn 'Umar, *Tafsiru'l-Qur'ani'l-Azim*, I–VIII, İstanbul, 1984.

Ibn Maja, Muhammad ibn Yazid al-Kazvini, *as-Sunan*, I–II, Daru'l-Kutubi'l-'Ilmiyya, Beirut.

Ibnu'l-Mubarak, 'Abdullah ibnu'l-Mubarak al-Marwazi, *az-Zuhd li-Ibn Mubarek*, Daru'l-Kutubi'l-'Ilmiyya, Beirut.

Malik ibn Anas, Abu 'Abdillah al-Asbahi, *al-Muwatta'*, I–II, Daru'l-Hadith, Cairo, 1993.

Al-Muhasibi, Abu 'Abdillah Harith ibn Asad, *ar-Ri'aya li-Huquqi'llah*, Cairo, 1970.

Mulla Jami', Mawlana Nuru'd-Din 'Abdu'r-Rahman ibn Ahmad, *Lujjatu'l-Asrar*, (trans.), İstanbul, 1897.

——, *Baharistan*, Ankara, 1945.

——, *Nafahatu'l-Uns*, Tehran, n.d.

(al-)Munawi, Muhammad ibn Mad'uvv ibn 'Abdi'r-Rauf, *Faydu'l-Qadir Sharhu Jami'us-Saghir*, Maktabatu't-Tijratiyyati'-Kubra, Egypt, 1356 AH.

Muslim, Abu'l-Nusayn al-Hajjaj an-Naysaburi, *Sahihu Muslim*, I–IV, Daru Ihyai't-Turathi'l-'Arabi, Beirut.

Mustafa Fevzi ibn Numan, *Mizanu'l-'Irfan*, İstanbul.

(al-)Muttaqi'l-Hindi, 'Alau'd-Din 'Ali, _Kanzu'l-ʿUmmal fi Sunani'l-Aqwal wa'l-Afʿal_, I–VIII, Beirut, 1985.

(an-)Nasa'i, Abu 'Abdur-Rahman Ahmad ibn Shu'ayb, _as-Sunan_, I–VIII, Maktabatu'l-Matbu'ati'l-Islamiyya, Aleppo, 1986.

Nursi, Bediüzzaman Said, _Sözler_ (The Words), Şahdamar Yayınları, İstanbul, 2005.

——, _Mektubat_ (The Letters), Şahdamar Yayınları, İstanbul, 2005.

——, _Mesnevi-i Nuriye_ (al-Mathnawi an-Nuri), Şahdamar Yayınları, İstanbul, 2005.

Qadi 'Iyad, Abu'l-Fadl 'Iyad ibn Musa, _ash-Shifa fi Taʿrifi Huquqi Mustafa_, I–II. Daru'l-Arqam, Beirut.

(al-)Qurtubi, Muhammad ibn Ahmad ibn Abi Bakir, _al-Jami' li-Ahkami'l-Qur'an_, I–XX, Daru'sh-Sha'b, Cairo, 1372 AH.

(al-)-Qushayri, Abu'l-Qasim 'Abdu'l-Karim, _ar-Risalatu'l-Qushayriya fi ʿUlumi'l-Tasawwuf_, Cairo, 1972.

(ar-)-Rabbani, Imam Ahmad Faruqi as-Sarhandi, _al-Maktubat_, 1277 AH / 1861 CE.

(ar-)-Rumi, Mawlana Jalalu'd-Din, _Mathnawi-i Kabir_, I–VI, Istanbul, n.d.

——, _Diwan-i Kabir_. I–VI, 1957.

——, _Gulshan-i Tawhid_, İstanbul.

Sarı Abdullah Efendi, _Samaratu'l-Fuad fi Mabda wa'l-Maʿad_, İstanbul.

Shabustari, Sa'dud-Din Mahmud ibn 'Abdu'l-Karim ibn Yahya, _Gulshan-i Raz_, Ankara, 1972.

(ash-)Sharani, 'Abdu'l-Wahhab, _at-Tabaqatu'l-Kubra_, Egypt, 1299 AH / 1881 CE.

(at-)Tabarani, Abu'l-Qasim Muhammad ibn Ahmad, _al-Muʿjamu's-Saghir_, I–II, al-Maktabatu'l-Islami, Beirut/Amman, 1985.

——, _al-Muʿjamu'l-Awsat_, Daru'l-Haramayn, Cairo, 1415 AH.

——, _al-Muʿjamu'l-Kabir_, Maktabatu'l-Ulumi wa'l-Hikam, Mosul, 1404 AH.

(at-)Tirmidhi, Abu 'Isa Muhammad ibn 'Isa, _al-Jami'us-Sahih_, I–IV, Daru Ihyai't-Turathi'l-'Arabi, Beirut.

Vehbi, Mehmed Vehbi Sünbülzade, _Lutfiye-i Vehbi_, Bedir Yayınevi, İstanbul, 1996.

Yazıcıoğlu Mehmed Efendi, _Muhammediye_, İstanbul.

INDEX

A

Aaron (Prophet), 142

'Abdullah ibn 'Abbas, 163

'Abdullah ibn 'Umar, 163

'Abdu'l-Qahir al-Baghdadi, 155

Abraham (Prophet), 54, 95, 112, 142, 148

Absorption; rank of, 106

Abu 'Ali ad-Daqqaq, 57

Abu Bakr ash-Shibli, 40

Abu Bakr ibnu'l-'Arabi, 155

Abu Hurayra, 163, 165-166

Abu Ishaq az-Zajjaj, 155

Adam (Prophet), 54, 95, 98, 100, 108, 134, 189

Ahmad ibn Ahmad Zarruq, 157

akhfa ("the more private"), 48

'Ali ibn Abi Talib, 12-13, 57, 63, 156, 163, 191, 193

al-Amadu'l-Aqsa', 155

'Arsh (The Supreme Throne of God), 75, 81; as the first arena where God Almighty's Grandeur and Sovereignty are manifested, 79; as the arena of the first manifestation of Divine will and command, 75; as the Supreme Throne of Life, 82; as the Supreme Throne of Livelihood, 82; as a mirror to overall Divine manifestation, 80; as a veil before His Attributes, 84; as the arena where God manifests His religious commands and His commands for creation and the operation of the universe as the Lord of the worlds, 76; as a combination of the Divine Names the First, the Last, the All-Outward, and the All-Inward, 81; God's establishing Himself on, 76-78; *'Arshu'r-Rahman* (The Supreme Throne of the All-Merciful), 87

'arshiya (the spiral way and curves of ascension), 75

al-Asma' wa's-Sifat, 155

annihilation; in God, 40; in the guide, 5; in the Will of the Lord, 7

Anthropomorphists (*Mujassima*), 152

Arabic, 40-41, 133, 142

ar-Rabbani, 104, 111-113, 159

Ash'aris, 140, 144

ash-Shibli, 40

Asma'ullahi'l-Husna, 155-157

(Divine) attraction, 22, 24, 54; toward God, 14; way of, 14

(Divine) Attributes, 76, 79-80, 84, 87, 100, 115-117, 119, 121, 123, 125, 127, 129-131, 133, 135, 137, 139, 141, 143, 145,

147, 149, 151-153, 164; as the veils of the Divine Essence, 115; Essential, 124, 126, 129-131, 133; Positive or Affirmative, 123-124, 130, 132-133, 158; of Action, 124; of Exemption, 124-127, 130-132, 158, 167; of Glory, 43, 54, 56, 59, 62, 68, 70, 76, 79-80, 90, 104, 111, 113, 115-121, 123-125, 127, 129, 131, 133, 135, 137, 139, 141, 143, 145, 147, 149, 151, 153, 160, 170; of Majesty and Grace, 133, 154, 159; of Glory as being designated as Attributes of Perfection, 115; of *Baqa* (Eternal Permanence), 129; of *Basar* (Sight), 137; of *Hayah* (Life), 133; of *Ibda'* (Originating Uniquely), 145, 146; of *Ihya* (giving life), 147; of *'Ilm* (Knowledge), 134; of *Imata* (causing to die), 147; of *Insha'* (Producing), 145, 146; of *Irada* (Will), xi, 5-7, 67, 70, 78, 85, 87, 99, 104-106, 109, 116-117, 132-135, 138-140, 143-144, 165, 168, 175, 184; of *Kalam* (Speech), 67, 100, 121, 133-134, 141-143; of *Khalq*, (Creation), 144; of *Muhalafatun lil-hawadith* (Being Unlike the Created), 126, 131-132; of *Qidam* (Having No Beginning), 129; of *Qiyam bi-nefsihi* (Self-Subsistence), 132; of *Qudra* (Power), 140; of *Sam'a* (Hearing), 136; of *Takwin* (Making

Exist), 143-144, 146; of *Tar-ziq* (Providing), 148; of *Wah-daniyya* (Oneness), 127; of *Wu-jud*, 126

Awhadu'd-Din 'Ali Anwari, 12

Ayman Abdu'r-Razzaq, 156

Aziz Mahmud Hudai, 111

B

batil (falsehood), 56

al-Bayhaqi, 58, 109, 156

al-Baytu'l-'Izza (the House of Honor), 92

al-Baytu'l-Ma'mur (the Prosperous House), 79, 90-93

Bediüzzaman, Said Nursi, xii, 81

al-Bidaya wa'n-Nihaya, 79, 156

C

certainty, 19, 25-26, 32, 37, 42-43, 46, 184, 186; of experience, 26; of knowledge, 26; of observation, 19, 26

Companions; of the Prophet, xiv, 29, 63

company; of God, 20, 24

Comparers (*Mushabbiha*), 152

D

David (Prophet), 34, 95, 142

dervish, 5, 39

desertion, 10

Diwan-i Kabir, 73, 193

E

Edirne, viii

Emir Muhammed, 40

Erzurum, vii, 8, 30, 66, 77, 83, 125, 138, 167

Eve, 100

F

Fakhru'd-Din ar-Razi, 155

farsh (the ground), 75

farshiya (the spiral way or curves of descent), 75

Flood, the, 91

Foundation of Journalists and Writers, ix

free will, 5-7, 32, 48, 94, 108, 131, 139-140, 159, 175, 179

G

al-Ghazzali, 35, 155, 159

Gospel, 95

guide (spiritual), ix, xi-xii, 4-9, 12-15, 18, 29-30, 33, 58, 111-112, 114, 176, 179

H

Hafiz ash-Shirazi, 180

al-Halimi, 155

al-Hallaj, Husayn ibn Mansur, 41

Hamid Ahmad Tahir, 156

haqaiq (truths), 59

Haqani, Afzalu'd-Din Ibrahim Badil ibn Ali, 20

haqiqa (essence, the genuine), 56

haqq (the truth), 56

heart, vii-viii, xiv, 4, 6-9, 11-12, 15-16, 18, 20-21, 25, 31-34, 36-38, 40-42, 44-50, 52-55, 58, 61, 71, 73, 81-83, 91-92, 127, 159, 161-162, 166, 175-176, 183, 185, 187-188; as the house of God, 9, 12, 34; people of, 41

Hidden Treasure, 48, 50, 52-53, 108-109

Hikmah (science of Ma'rifah), xiii

himma (endeavor), viii, 22, 31-33, 47, 57, 91, 117, 181

Hoja Hasan Tahsin, 60, 165

human being; as the miniature and the most precious copy of the whole universe, 63

I

Ibn Kathir, 79, 88, 90, 156, 192

Ibn Qayyim al-Jawziya, 156

Ibnu'l-Farid, 41

Ibrahim Haqqi of Erzurum, 30, 66, 77, 83, 125, 138, 167

Ilyas (Prophet), 21

Imadu'd-Din Nasimi, 40

Imam Malik, 78-79, 163

intimacy; with God, 34-35, 44; with mentioning of God, 34

Isaac (Prophet), 142

Ishmael (Prophet), 142

Ismail Haqqi Bursavi, 61, 103, 177, 192

istawa, 75-76, 78

İzmir, viii

J

Jacob (Prophet), 142

Jahmiyya, 131, 152

al-Jamiʿ li-Asma'il-Husna, 156

Jesus (Prophet), 54, 119, 134, 142; Messiah, 96, 119

Job (Prophet), 142

Jonah (Prophet), 142

journeying, xi-xii, 2-4, 7, 10-12, 14, 16, 19-24, 26, 32, 37, 41-42, 44-45, 52-54, 56, 61, 73, 92, 119, 175, 177, 182, 188; spiritual, 3, 24, 37, 52, 56, 119, 177; from God, 177; "in" and "with or in the company of God", 20, 25, 177; toward God, 27, 42; meeting with God as the final point or destination of, 23

Junayd al-Baghdadi, 3, 40, 72

K

Ka'ba, 61, 82, 87, 90-92; being the House of God as an expression of its supreme relation to God Almighty, 87

Kashfu'l-Ma'na an Sirri Asma'illahi'l-Husna, 156

al-Khadr, 21

khafi ("the private"), 48

al-Kitabu'l-Athna' fi Sharhi Asma'ulla-hi'l-Husna, 156

knowledge, viii, xi, xiii, 1, 3, 9, 16, 19, 22, 24-30, 35-36, 42-43, 45-50, 54, 56-57, 59-64, 67, 69, 71, 74, 76, 80, 82-83, 86, 90-95, 106, 109, 116-117, 121, 124, 135-137, 148, 152, 154, 158-161, 167, 176, 178-179, 181-185; of Divine Attributes and Essential Qualities, 28; of God (*Ma'rifah*), xi, xiii, 3, 16, 19, 22, 24-25, 27-30, 35-36, 42-43, 45,

48, 54, 56, 59, 74, 106, 154, 161, 176, 178-179, 182, 184-185; of God's Acts, 28; of the truth, 28; as the Divine Attribute Whose area of comprehension is the broadest, 134;

Kur'an'da Uluhiyet, 157

Kursiyy (God's Supreme Seat) 79; as an arena of the manifestation of Divine Sovereignty and Rule, 87; as a platform for God's practices as the Lord, 84; as the horizon of the manifestation of Divine Power, 87; as the realm where God's commands are manifested and implemented, 83, 85; as the arena of the manifestation of all attributes of existence in the corporeal realm, 85; *al-Kursiyyu'r-Rabbani* (The Supreme Seat of the Lord), 87

L

Lawa'mi'ul-Bayyinat, 155

Lawhun Mahfuz (the Supreme Preserved Tablet), 82, 92-95, 97-101, 103-104, 107; as another name for the Divine Knowledge, 93; as the Mother Book, 97; as the Manifest Record, 97

life, 67, 70, 82, 103, 107, 109, 116, 118, 121-122, 130, 132-134, 144, 147, 158, 165-166; as the most comprehensive of all the Divine Attributes of Glory, 118

al-Lujja, 32

M

Makka; the Secure Town of, 91

al-Maqsadu'l-Athna' fi Sharhi Asma'ul-lahi'l-Husna, 155, 157

Maturidis, 140, 143-144

al-Minhaj, 33

al-Minhaj fi Shu'abil-Iman, 155

Mizanu'l-'Irfan, 45, 192

Moses (Prophet), 21, 54, 95, 101, 119, 142

Muhammad (Prophet), x, xiii, 18, 33, 35, 37, 46, 50, 53, 55, 57, 63, 88-89, 92, 96, 100, 102-103, 108-110, 112-114, 118, 140, 149, 153, 155-157, 162, 168, 177, 188, 191-193; Ahmad, 32, 96, 104, 112, 156, 183, 191-193; King of Prophets, 86; Last Messenger, 154; Master of Creation, 18, 38, 94, 96, 108, 112, 117, 119, 160; unequalled hero of whole-hearted devotion, 33; his spirit as the first of the creative identifications, 108; as the Seal of the Mission of Prophethood, 54, 61, 74, 89; as the Inaugurator and Seal of Prophethood, 61, 74; Pride of humankind, 86; spirit of, 108-109; Truth of, 103, 112-113; as the purpose for the creation of the universe, 109; Honor of Humankind and the Peerless of Time and Space, 89; as the ultimate purpose for the existence of the universe, 113; Family of, 13, 166

Muhammad ibn Sa'id al-Busiri, 113

Muhammed Ali Hilmi Dede, 4

Muhammed İbrahim Efendi, 157

Muhammed Lutfi Efendi, 8, 19, 28

Muhyi'd-Din ibnu'l-'Arabi, xiii, 5, 156

Mulla Jami', 103, 120, 192

murid (the one who wills), xiv-xv, 3-10, 13, 15, 24, 31

Mu'tazila, 131, 152

N

(Divine) Names; indicating Divine Acts, 171; indicating the Divine Essence, 168; Foundational, 173; of Grace, 168, 174; of Majesty, 168, 174; manifestation of, 1-2, 4, 88, 104, 111, 115, 121, 159; originating in Divine Attributes of Glory, 170; Allah as the Greatest or All-Supreme Name, 62-63, 69, 157, 161, 166, 168; *Hu* ("He"–the pronoun used with God), as being God's All-Supreme Name, 68; for the All-Beautiful Names of God see pp. 154-174.

Niyazi-i Mısri, 15

Noah (Prophet), 91, 95, 142

P

People of the Cloak, 13

progression; spiritual, xiii

Psalms, 95, 142

Ptolemy, 86

Q

Qur'an; as a manifestation of Divine Speech, 142
al-Qurtubi, 78, 156
al-Qushayri, 157

R

Realm; of corporeality, 175; of Ideal Forms or Representations, 103; of spirits, 175; of the Transcendental Manifestation of Divine Attributes and Names, 175; of the Transcendental Manifestation of Divine Commands, 175; of the Transcendental Manifestation of Divinity, 175; of the Unseen, 98-99
rizq (provision), 148
Rumi, Mawlana Jalalu'd-Din, 39-40, 73, 185, 192-193

S

as-Sa'di, 156
salik (the initiate), 1, 3-4, 7, 13-16, 19-22, 24, 28-29, 31, 46, 61
Salmanu'l-Farisi, 163
Sayyid Sharif al-Jurjani, 62
self-purification, xi
Seyyid Mir Hamza Nigari, 73
Sharhi Asma'i'l-Husna, 157
Sharhu Asma'illahi'l-Husna, 157
Sidra; marking the farthest boundary of the realm of creation, 88
Sidratu'l-Muntaha (the Lote-tree of the furthest limit), 79, 88-90, 92; as a blessed tree which exists to the right of God's Supreme Throne, 88
sir ("the secret"), 48
Solomon (Prophet), 142
Suat Yıldırım, 157
subsistence; by and with God, 40, 92
Sufism; as a life-long process of spiritual development, xi
as-Suhrawardi, Shihabu'd-Din Abu Hafs 'Umar ibn 'Abdullah, 41
Süleyman Çelebi, 89, 110

T

ta'ayyun (identification), 103; as Existence, 106; as Knowledge, 106
Tablet; of Devoted Servanthood, 101; of Divine Destiny and Decree, 97; of Effacement and Confirmation, 95, 97-100; of Judgment, 100; of Light, 100; of Wisdom, 100
Tafsirul-Asma'ul-Husna, 155
talib (the seeker), 1, 3-5, 15
taqwa (piety and righteousness), 185
tariqa (spiritual path), 56
Ten Commandments, 101
Torah, 96
Touba tree, 110
traveler, 1-2, 4, 7-13, 15-18, 21, 24, 27, 31, 35, 42-43, 89, 176-177, 182; of the Sufi path, 188; to the Ultimate Truth, 2-3, 7, 9-10, 59, 177; toward God, 35, 42-43
Turkey, vii-ix, 15, 29-30, 40, 60-61, 89, 111, 157, 160-161, 188

U

'Umar ibnu'l-Farid, 41
Unbreakable Rope, 2

W

Wahdatu'l-Wujud; doctrine of, xiii
Wahidiya (Divine Unity), xiii, 5,
    60, 68-71, 100-101, 105-106,
    117, 120, 126, 137, 158, 169,
    176, 178; of Divinity, 70-71; of
    Lordship, 70-71

wasil (the one who has attained), xiv-
    xv, 3, 24, 34, 37, 186

Y

Yazıcızade Muhammed Efendi, 188
Yunus Emre, 29, 161
Yusuf 'Ali, 156

Z

Ziya Pasha, 160